Algebra, Data, and Probability Explorations for Middle School

A GRAPHICS CALCULATOR APPROACH

Graham A. Jones and Roger Day

Dale Seymour Publications®
Menlo Park, California

Acknowledgments

We wish to thank Jenni Cindel, Lynn Glassmaker, Jennifer Gula, Marion Jones, and James Tarr for their many valuable contributions to this book.

Credits

Data for Figures 1 and 2 on page 51 and Data Set 4 on page 142: *HitsWorld*, 1996 (URL: http://www.hitsworld.com)
Data for the graph on page 93: *USA Today*, 1996
Data for Data Set 7 on page 145: *Performance Magazine*, 1994 and 1995
Windsurfer Race Game: Developed by Laura van Zoest and Roberta Walker

Project Editor: Joan Gideon
Production Coordinators: Shannon Miller and Amy Changar
Art and composition: A.W. Kingston Publishing Services
Text and cover design: Christy Butterfield
Cover art: Ed Taber

Published by Dale Seymour Publications®, an imprint of Addison Wesley Longman Inc.

Dale Seymour Publications
2725 Sand Hill Road
Menlo Park, CA 94025
Customer Service: 800-872-1100

Order Number DS21807

ISBN 1-57232-269-1

2 3 4 5 6 7 8 9 10-ML-01 00 99

Contents

Student Activities

MODULE 2: DATA

Student Activities

MODULE 3: PROBABILITY

Student Activities

Appendices

Glossary

Introduction

The National Council of Teachers of Mathematics *Curriculum and Evaluation Standards for School Mathematics* (1989) focuses attention on new goals for school mathematics. In particular, the Standards put great stress on four mathematical processes: problem solving, communication, reasoning, and making connections. They also emphasize new and emerging content areas for middle-school students, such as algebra, data analysis, and probability. This book explores these three content areas using the mathematical processes advocated in the Standards. The book also captures another major thrust of the Standards—the application of appropriate technology to problem-solving activities.

The book has three modules. *Module 1: Algebra* focuses on patterns and relationships as vehicles for developing algebraic reasoning with middle-school students. *Module 2: Data* emphasizes making sense of data through organizing, displaying, and interpreting data in various ways. *Module 3: Probability* incorporates simulations and analysis to determine both experimental and theoretical probabilities associated with real-world problems.

The book offers special flexibility. Each module can be used as a replacement unit or as a supplemental unit. As replacement units, the modules can be used to introduce and develop emerging topics not typically emphasized in traditional textbooks. On the other hand, the book can be used to supplement reform-based programs such as *The Connected Mathematics Project.*

Graphics calculators are used both to build concepts and as a tool. While the TI–80 is referred to explicitly in the book, you can adapt the materials to any appropriate graphics calculator.

Special Features for the Teacher

In each module of *Algebra, Data, and Probability Explorations for Middle School,* preceding the Student Activities are the following helpful features for teachers.

- *Module Overview.* The overview identifies the scope and direction of the module, as well as expectations to be set for students.

- *Outline of Key Mathematical Ideas.* This chart shows the mathematical topic for each activity.

- *Content Background.* This section uses a problem-solving approach to present the mathematical content for the module. It is for you to refer to if you want to review a concept.

- *Implementation Notes and Solutions.* For each activity, this section provides specific instructional suggestions as well as solutions to the three parts of the problems: Investigate, Share, Extend.

Special Features for the Student

The student blackline master pages of each module incorporate these features.

- *Activities.* In order to meet the needs of diverse student backgrounds, each module offers three levels of Activities—Developing, Applying, and Challenging. To reflect new approaches to instruction, each activity contains four components.

A focus Problem is presented and students are guided to Investigate it, often in several ways. Students Share investigations in written or oral form with the class or small group. The problem in Extend is designed to build further on the mathematical ideas of the activity.

- *Data Sets.* Located at the back of the book, Data Sets are provided for activities that require them. However, you are also encouraged to generate their own data sets.

- *Calculator Helps.* When required, Calculator Helps are highlighted in the Investigate section of an Activity. The Calculator Help pages, placed at the back of the book, explain and illustrate specific TI-80 graphics calculator procedures used in the modules.

Module 1

ALGEBRA

Overview

The activities in *Module 1: Algebra* emphasize the exploration and investigation of numerical and geometrical patterns arising from real-world settings. This exploration is intended to lead to the study of relationships that are represented by variables and functions. In essence, the goal is to move students from arithmetic reasoning to algebraic reasoning.

The expected outcomes of the *Module 1: Algebra* are that students will be able to

- discover and describe patterns

- describe and represent relationships using variables

- construct tables and graphs of relationships using a graphics calculator

- make connections between relationships, their tables, and their graphs

- solve algebraic equations and identify equivalent expressions

This module can be used as a replacement unit or as a supplemental unit. When used as a replacement unit, we encourage you to have students explore most of the Developing activities (1-1 to 1-22) in sequence. After the initial exploration of several patterns (Activities 1-1 to 1-6), the activities progressively investigate linear relationships (Activities 1-7 to 1-19), quadratic relationships (Activities 1-20 to 1-22), and exponential relationships (Activities 1-27, 1-28). Some of the problem settings are rich enough to enable you to build additional activities to meet student needs. This approach would allow you to use some of the Applying and the Challenging activities as projects, or alternatively, to use them in subsequent years. Although some of you may decide to save quadratic and exponential relationships for use in later grade levels, we believe there is value in exposing students to both linear and non-linear relationships.

If the module serves as a supplemental unit, you could use the following sequence to advantage: Applying activities 1-23 to 1-25 (linear relationships); Developing activities 1-19 to 1-22 and Applying activity 1-26 (quadratic relationships); Applying activities 1-27 and 1-28 (exponential relationships). If you want to develop algebraic reasoning using symbolic expressions, Developing activities 1-14 to 1-18 are very useful. The Challenging activities would be most appropriate as assessment projects.

Use the content background (pages 3–6) for your own review of algebra concepts and vocabulary. Information on presenting the student activities (pages 19–47) begins on page 7.

DEVELOPING ACTIVITIES	KEY MATHEMATICAL IDEAS
1-1 Bouncing a Tennis Ball	variables and patterns
1-2 Graphing the Tennis-Ball Bounces	scatter plots
1-3 Growth in the Number of Bounces	rate of change
1-4 Packing the Tennis Balls	variables and patterns
1-5 Graphing the Tennis-Ball-Packing Data	scatter plots
1-6 Growth in the Number of Tennis Balls	rate of change
1-7 Buying Regular Gasoline	variables and linear patterns
1-8 A Cost Pattern for Regular Gasoline	linear relationships
1-9 Regular Gasoline and Motor Oil	linear relationships
1-10 A Cost Pattern for Gasoline and Oil	linear relationships
1-11 Graphing the Cost Pattern for Gasoline and Oil	graphing linear relationships
1-12 Patterns for Four Types of Gasoline	slope and rate of change
1-13 When Does Gerda Catch Peter?	intersections of linear relationships
1-14 Using the Two-Seat Ski Lift	linear relationships
1-15 Graphing the Two-Seat Ski Lift	graphing linear relationships
1-16 Simplifying Expressions	equivalent expressions
1-17 Did Max Simplify the Expression?	equivalent expressions
1-18 Mixed Rows on the Three-Seat Ski Lift	equivalent expressions
1-19 Valentine's Day Fund Raiser	linear relationships
1-20 How Much Profit?	quadratic relationships
1-21 Graphing the Profit	graphing quadratic relationships
1-22 Does the Profit Change at a Constant Rate?	rates of change

APPLYING ACTIVITIES	KEY MATHEMATICAL IDEAS
1-23 The Lemonade Stand	linear relationships
1-24 Finding the Lemonade-Stand Profit	equivalent expressions
1-25 Economy Class	equivalent expressions
1-26 A Bowling Tournament	quadratic relationships
1-27 Brent's Savings Plan	exponential relationships
1-28 Graphing Brent's Savings Plan	graphing exponential relationships

CHALLENGING ACTIVITIES	KEY MATHEMATICAL IDEAS
1-29 Softball Fallout	quadratic relationships
1-30 Fruit Juice and Cookies	exponential relationships

Content Background

Linear Relationships The following problems and their solutions cover the key concepts of linear relationships that are explored in this module. Problems 1 and 2 refer to Data Set 2: Colleen's Tennis-Ball-Bounce Data (page 140), repeated here for your convenience.

Colleen's Tennis-Ball-Bounce Data

Elapsed Time (seconds)	Total Number of Bounces
0	0
20	24
40	48
60	72
80	96
100	120
120	144

Problem 1 Describe some of the patterns involving elapsed time and total number of bounces. If x represents the elapsed time and y represents the total number of bounces, find a relationship between y and x.

Solution Here are some patterns to observe.

(a) The total number of bounces increases by 24 for each 20-second time period.

(b) The total number of bounces is always equal to 1.2 times the elapsed time.

Hence, the second pattern shows that $y = 1.2x$, a linear relationship with a straight-line graph where x represents the elapsed time in seconds and y represents the total number of bounces.

Notes

1. Students should be encouraged to look for patterns both within data values for each variable and between the variables. The relationships within the variables reveal that there is a uniform increase in the total number of bounces for each 20 seconds of elapsed time.

2. In this problem, y is said to be the dependent variable because the total number of bounces depends on the elapsed time. Because y depends on x, we say that x is the independent variable.

Problem 2 Find the slope of the graph of the linear relationship $y = 1.2x$.

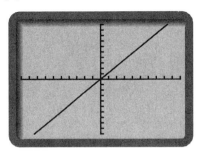

Solution The screen shows the graph of $y = 1.2x$. Because the slope of the line is uniform, or constant, it can be found from any pair of points in the relationship. For example, using (20, 24) and (80, 96), the slope is $\dfrac{96-24}{80-20} = 1.2$.

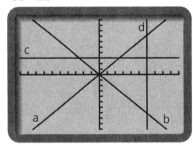

Notes

1. The slope of a line joining two points can be found by determining the ratio $\dfrac{\text{change in } y}{\text{change in } x}$. In the case above, the slope is positive, indicating that the line rises as you move from left to right as in line a. In other cases, the line has negative slope as in line b (falling from left to right); the line has a slope of zero as in line c (horizontal, with no change in y); or the line has no slope as in line d (vertical, with no change in x).

2. You will also notice the slope appears in the equation $y = 1.2x$ as the coefficient of x, or the number that multiplies x. In general, the equation of a straight line can be written in the form $y = mx + b$, where x is the independent variable, y is the dependent variable, m is a constant value that represents the slope, and b is a constant value representing the intercept of the y-axis, the y-value for $x = 0$. An intercept can also be thought of as the point at which the graph crosses an axis. For the equation $y = 1.2x$, the y-intercept is 0, since the line passes through the origin.

3. Because the slope is $\dfrac{\text{change in } y}{\text{change in } x}$, a slope of 1.2 represents the increase in the total number of bounces per one-second increase in elapsed time. In essence, the slope represents the rate of change in the dependent variable per unit change in the independent variable. In this case, the rate of change is 1.2 bounces per second.

Problem 3 Find an equation for the straight line that passes through the points (1, 2) and (3, 1).

Solution The slope of the line is $\dfrac{1-2}{3-1} = -0.5$. So the equation of the line has the form $y = -0.5x + b$, where b is yet to be determined.

Because (1, 2) lies on the line, it must satisfy the equation. Therefore, $2 = -0.5(1) + b$, resulting in the value $b = 2.5$.

The desired equation is $y = -0.5x + 2.5$.

Notes

1. In this module, students will generally find equations for relationships by exploring patterns. However, you will find it helpful, when generating examples or in checking students' work, to be able to find the equation of a straight line using the form $y = mx + b$.

2. The y-axis intercept for this line is 2.5. This indicates that the line passes through the point (0, 2.5).

Problem 4 Refer to Colleen's data set, and find the elapsed time when the total number of bounces is 60.

Solution While the problem can be solved in many ways, we present here a solution based on algebraic reasoning.

For these data, we know that $y = 1.2x$. Thus, when the total number of bounces is 60, $60 = 1.2x$, resulting in the value $x = 50$. After 50 seconds, the total number of bounces is 60.

Notes

1. In extending students' algebraic thinking, you will often find it helpful to build problems that can be modeled by equations such as the one in Problem 4. Another version is to ask students to find the total number of bounces when the elapsed time is 70 seconds. The associated equation is $y = 1.2(70)$.

2. You could also generate problems that lead to inequalities, such as: For what range of elapsed times is the total number of bounces less than 60? Based on the solution to Problem 4, the range is from 0 to 50 seconds ($0 \le x < 50$).

Non-Linear Relationships Non-linear relationships arise from many patterns in real-world problem settings. In this section, we investigate problems that lead to quadratic and exponential relationships. The characteristics of these relationships are explored by examining the corresponding graphs, tables, and equations. The quadratic and exponential relationships are also contrasted with linear relationships.

Problem 5 Naomi is building a rectangular pen for her hamsters. She has 10 feet of wire fencing to make the pen. If all of the fencing is to be used, find a relationship between the area of the pen and its length in feet.

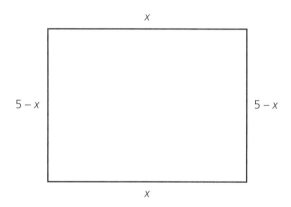

Solution Let x represent the length of the pen in feet. Because the perimeter of the pen is 10 feet, we know that half the perimeter (one length and one width) is 5 feet. This means that the width of the pen is $5 - x$, and the area is $x(5 - x)$.

Notes

1. While algebraic reasoning is easily used to find this relationship, encourage students to explore a problem like this by considering specific lengths, building tables, drawing diagrams of the corresponding rectangles, and looking for patterns.

2. The same relationship occurs if x represents the width of the hamster pen. This is because the sum of the length and the width is equal to half the perimeter.

Problem 6 Construct a graph and table for the relationship $Y1 = x(5 - x)$, where $Y1$ is the area of the hamster pen and x represents the length of the pen.

Solution The TI-80 gives the graph and table for the relationship $Y1 = x(5 - x)$ shown on page 5.

The shape of the graph is a curve, called a *parabola*, and we notice from both the table and the graph that $Y1$ does not change by a constant amount for equal changes in x. Unlike the graph of a straight line, the curve does not have a constant slope. In fact, the slope is positive for values of x between 0 and 2.5 and negative for values of x between 2.5 and 5.

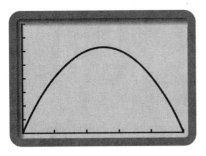

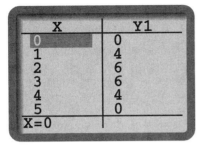

Notes

1. The relationship Y1 = x(5 − x), often written as Y1 = 5x − x², is called a *quadratic relationship* because the greatest power of the independent variable x is 2.

2. The graph of every quadratic relationship is a parabola. However, the parabola opens downward if the coefficient of x² is negative, as in the case above, or upward if the coefficient of x² is positive. This is shown here in the graph of Y2 = x² − 5x + 8.

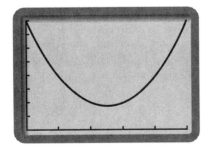

3. Observation of the graph of Y2 = x² − 5x + 8 also reveals that its y-intercept is 8; that is, it passes through the point (0, 8). Notice that Y1 = 5x − x² has a y-intercept of 0 because it has the equivalent form Y1 = 5x − x² + 0.

4. To summarize the properties outlined in notes 2 and 3, the graph of y = ax² + bx + c

   • opens upward if a > 0 and opens downward if a < 0

   • has a y-intercept of c

   It is also possible to show that changing the value of b simultaneously shifts the graph horizontally and vertically while the shape and the y-intercept remain unchanged.

Problem 7 Assuming that all 10 feet of fencing are used, what should be the dimensions of Naomi's hamster pen (see Problem 5) if the area is to be as large as possible?

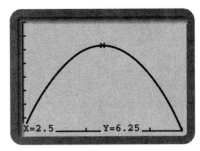

Solution From the solution to Problem 5, we know that the area of the pen is given by Y1 = x(5 − x), where Y1 is the area of the pen and x is its length. Using TRACE on the TI-80 graph of Y1 = x(5 − x), we can see that the value of Y1 increases from x = 0 to x = 2.5 and then decreases for values of x greater than 2.5. Hence the maximum value occurs when x = 2.5 and Y1 = 6.25, as illustrated in the screen. This tells us that the maximum area for a rectangular pen with perimeter 10 feet is 6.25 square feet.

Note

1. In Problem 6, we observed that the graph of the relationship Y1 = x(5 − x) = 5x − x² opened downward. We now recognize that this graph has a maximum value. By way of contrast, graphs of relationships such as Y2 = x² − 5x + 8 that open upward have a minimum value. Refer to the screen shown with the notes for Problem 6.

Problem 8 explores an exponential relationship.

Problem 8 The number of bluegills hatched from eggs in a fish-hatchery tank during a five-hour period is shown in the table.

Rate of Bluegill Hatching

Time in Hours	0	1	2	3	4	5
Total Number of Bluegills Hatched	1	2	4	8	16	32

If t is the time in hours and n is the number of bluegills hatched after t hours, find a relationship between n and t.

Solution The patterns within the values for each variable tell us that the number of bluegills doubles every hour. If we express the number of bluegills as powers of 2, as shown in the solution table on the next page, we can distinguish the pattern between the variables t and n. We notice that when the time is 2 hours, the number of bluegills is 4, or 2^2; when the time is 3 hours, the number of bluegills is 8, or 2^3; and so on. Hence the relationship between n and t is given by $n = 2^t$, where n is the total number of bluegills hatched after t hours.

Rate of Bluegill Hatching

Time (hours)	Total Number of Bluegills Hatched
0	$1 = 2^0$
1	$2 = 2^1$
2	$4 = 2^2$
3	$8 = 2^3$
4	$16 = 2^4$
5	$32 = 2^5$

Notes

1. The relationship $n = 2^t$ is called an *exponential relationship* because the independent variable is an exponent, or power, in this relationship. In this expression, the *base*, or number being raised to a power, is 2. In the expression 2^t, 2 is said to be the *growth factor* or the *growth rate*.

2. The value of n doubles for each unit change in t. In contrast to the linear relationship $y = 1.2x$ (Problem 1), which changes by 1.2 bounces for each unit change in x (called an *additive change*), the exponential relationship, $n = 2^t$, doubles for each unit change in t (called a *multiplicative change*).

Problem 9 Construct a graph and a table for the relationship $n = 2^t$, where n is the total number of bluegills hatched after t hours.

Solution Using the TI-80, we use Y3 to represent the dependent variable n and x to represent the independent variable t. The graph and table for the relationship Y3 = 2^x are shown here. The shape of the graph is characteristic of exponential relationships. It is clear that Y3 does not change by a constant amount for equal changes in x.

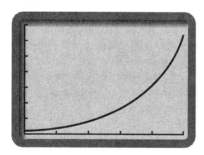

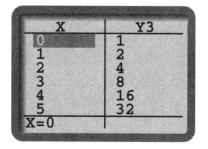

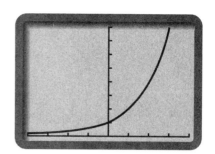

Notes

1. Although the graph of Y2 = 2^x was plotted for only positive values of x, the graph of Y3 = 2^x is plotted here for both positive and negative values of x. Notice that Y3 is always positive even though it approaches zero for large negative values of x.

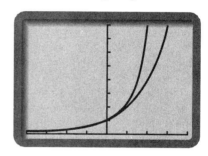

2. The graph of Y4 = 3^x has the same characteristic exponential shape as the graph of Y3 = 2^x but for positive values of x is steeper because its growth factor 3 is larger than the growth factor 2. Notice that the graphs of both Y3 = 2^x and Y4 = 3^x shown here pass through the point (0, 1); that is, they have y-intercepts of 1.

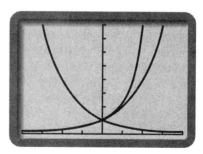

3. Although the graph of Y5 = $\left(\frac{1}{2}\right)^x$ has the same characteristic exponential shape as the graph of Y3 = 2^x and Y4 = 3^x, it is different in that it decreases as x increases. Because of this we say that $\frac{1}{2}$ is the *decay factor* rather than the growth factor.

You might also observe that the graphs of Y3 = 2^x and Y5 = $\left(\frac{1}{2}\right)^x$ are symmetrical about the y-axis as shown in the last screen.

Implementation Notes and Solutions

Developing Activities

ACTIVITY 1-1 (p. 18)   VARIABLES AND PATTERNS

Bouncing a Tennis Ball

Students' data will vary for the number of times they can bounce and catch a tennis ball in 2 minutes, but the data should be reasonably linear. Different surfaces, for example, carpet, concrete, or tiles, will produce different bounce heights, and this could affect the number of times students bounce the ball. This is meant to be an exploratory activity, but students might notice that the total number of bounces increases by about the same number every 10 seconds. They might also recognize that each time value can be multiplied by the same number (a constant) to give the corresponding total number of bounces. This is an appropriate time for you to review the concepts of variable, dependent variable, and independent variable. In the Extend, answers will vary. The prediction for 4 minutes can be made by using one of the patterns found earlier.

ACTIVITY 1-2 (p. 19)   SCATTER PLOTS

Graphing the Tennis-Ball Bounces

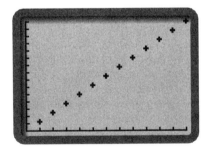

The scatter plot shows that the data points (p. 140) are strongly linear; that is, they can easily be located on a straight line. The two different patterns identified in the Share are very important. Our experience suggests that students often look at the pattern associated within the total number of bounces, but they are less likely to look at the pattern between elapsed time and total number of bounces. It is this latter pattern (number of cumulative bounces equals time multiplied by 1.2) that will drive the expressing of an algebraic relationship, or an equation, between the two variables. Asking students to write about the patterns helps them clarify their thinking. For the Extend, Colleen's data do not reveal any different patterns. The total number of bounces increases by 24 every 20 seconds, or 12 every 10 seconds, and for any given time the total number of bounces can be found by multiplying the time by 1.2. The emphasis on seeking patterns within and across variables will be important throughout this module.

ACTIVITY 1-3 (p. 20)   RATE OF CHANGE

Growth in the Number of Tennis-Ball Bounces

This activity should pull together the initial ideas of variables and patterns. A number of students will have already determined that the total number of bounces increases by 24 every 20 seconds, so the rate of increase is 1.2 bounces per second. This observation will provide a valuable opportunity for students to discuss slope and constant slope. As a follow-up or supporting activity, you might find it helpful for students to measure the slope of a slide in the playground, a set of stairs, or a walking ramp. It is especially important that students understand the units of measure, such as bounces per second, when they discuss rate and slope.

In the Extend, the scatter plot for Lindsay's grandfather is essentially the same as Data Set 1: Tennis-Ball-Bounce Data for the first 60 seconds, but then tends to flatten out, presumably as Lindsay's grandfather was tiring. Hence the scatter plot tends to be a straight line with constant slope for the first 60 seconds and then a curve whose slope is not constant after that. Some students may even argue that the scatter plot is curved from the start and that the slope is not constant. This is fine, provided that they justify their response.

ACTIVITY 1-4 (p. 21)   VARIABLES AND PATTERNS

Packing the Tennis Balls

It would be helpful to let students set up this task using boxes of appropriate sizes. They could make the boxes with paper. If the boxes are constructed, students will more easily recognize the variables in the problem. They should recognize that the dependent variable is the number of tennis balls in the box and the independent variable is the side length of the box's square base measured in tennis-ball units. Students should again be encouraged to look for patterns both within and between the two variables in the table that they produce. While there are interesting patterns within the values for each variable, it is the pattern between the variables that reveals that the number of tennis balls is the square of the side length in tennis-ball units. The table entries should be 1–1, 2–4, 3–9, 4–16, 5–25, 6–36, 7–49, 8–64, 9–81, 10–100, 11–121, 12–144, 13–169, 14–196, 15–225, 16–256, 17–289, 18–324, 19–361, and 20–400. Therefore, in the Extend, 1600 tennis balls correspond to a square box of side length 40 tennis-ball units.

Graphing the Tennis-Ball-Packing Data

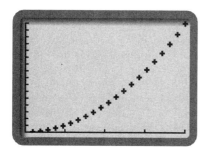

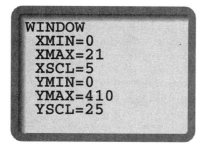

have the same general shape as the first but will not be as steep. Students might see this very effectively by showing the two scatter plots simultaneously on the TI-80. They can do this by using STAT PLOT1 and STAT PLOT2. A careful perusal of the plot, using inches as the independent variable, will reveal a step function with the same general shape as the original. Teachers might like to encourage some students to explore this new relationship in more depth.

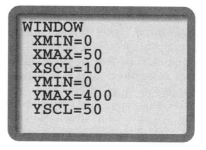

When students have constructed the scatter plot for the Packing the Tennis Balls data, they will notice that the points have the shape of a curve known as a *parabola*. Actually, the graph presents the curve for only the positive *x*-values. The additional number of tennis balls, per unit increase in the side of the box, grows quite rapidly. When the side length grows from 2 to 3 tennis-ball units, the increase in the number of tennis balls in a box is 5 (from 4 to 9). By way of contrast, an increase in side length from 9 to 10 units generates an increase of 19 (from 81 to 100) in the number of balls in a box.

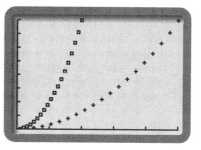

Growth in the Number of Tennis Balls

Rate of change, or slope, is a vital concept in algebra and other areas of mathematics. It would be especially valuable to have students regularly look at rate and slope and their units of measure throughout this module. The change in number of tennis balls per unit increase in side length grows rapidly (1, 3, 5, . . ., 37, 39). Unlike the rate investigated in Activity 1-3: Growth in the Number of Tennis-Ball Bounces, it is clearly not constant. The relationship between the number of tennis balls and the side length of the box in inches does produce an algebraic relationship:

$y = \left(\dfrac{x}{2.5}\right)^2$, and this relationship allows for various

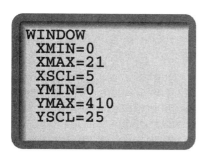

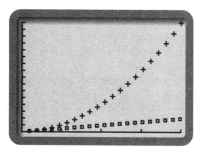

The Extend provides an interesting challenge. Students will need to measure the diameter of a tennis ball. It is approximately 2.5 inches. The plot they produce will

rates of increase to be calculated. However, these rates have limited meaning in terms of packing the tennis balls. For example, an increase from 1 to 2 inches in the side length of the box generates an increase from 0.16 to 0.64, or 0.48, tennis balls per inch. But pieces of tennis balls would not be packed. Some students may claim that an increase from 1 to 2 inches in the side length of the box generates no increase in the number of tennis balls.

Buying Regular Gasoline

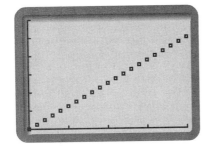

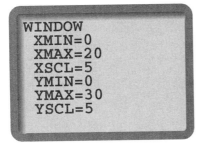

The activities in Module 1: Algebra now return to examine linear relationships and straight lines in more depth. The ultimate goal is for students to determine the equation of a straight line and to be able to find and interpret properties such as the slope and *y*-intercept. The task of finding a way to determine the cost when various numbers of gallons are purchased provides a key link between arithmetic and algebraic reasoning. It is important for students to write responses to such tasks. If they are having difficulty, try prompts such as, "What did you do to find the cost of 5 gallons? What did you do to find the cost of 20 gallons? Can you write in words what you did?" The earlier preparation in developing patterns both within and between the values of variables in tables should also be helpful for this problem. Students can solve the Extend in more than one way. One way is to find the difference in total costs for 15 gallons: $15 \times 1.31 - 15 \times 1.23 = 1.20$, or $1.20. Another way is to first find the difference in cost per gallon: $15 \times (1.31 - 1.23) = 1.20$, or $1.20.

A Cost Pattern for Regular Gasoline

Given the build-up of pattern development and writing, it is hoped students will be able to see that the relationship is 1.23 times *g*, or, in more usual notation, 1.23*g*. Notice that it is the pattern between the variables that generates the relationship. At some stage, you will want students to write this as an equation, such as, $C = 1.23g$, where *C* is the total cost and *g* is the number of gallons of regular gasoline purchased. Again, students could solve the Extend in a number of ways. Sylvia's approach attempts to stretch students' thinking toward more algebraic reasoning. In solving the equation, students could use various strategies, including guess and check, to find that Bev's dad bought 15 gallons of gasoline. Do not push students to formal solutions at this stage; rather, ask several students to share their solutions.

Regular Gasoline and Motor Oil

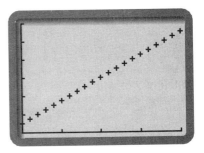

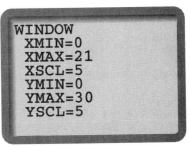

This activity involves a small extension of Activity 1-8. It is hoped that, by constructing the graph and the table, students will see that the graph does not pass through (0, 0) and that the cost of 0 gallons is $2, assuming Lindsay's dad purchases his usual quart of motor oil. It would also be a useful time to introduce the concept of *y*-intercept and relate it to what is essentially a fixed cost in this problem. Once again the task of determining the cost for various amounts of gasoline is important and needs to be addressed through writing and sharing. The Extend can be solved in various ways, including an approach similar to the one Sylvia used to solve the Extend in Activity 1-8. The solution is 15×0.25, or \$3.75.

ACTIVITY 1-10 (p. 27)   LINEAR RELATIONSHIPS

A Cost Pattern for Gasoline and Motor Oil

The patterns built in the previous activity should enable students to cross the bridge that leads to the result, $1.23x + 2$, as the total cost when Lindsay's dad purchases motor oil and *x* gallons of regular gasoline. This could also lead to the relationship $L = 1.23x + 2$, where *L* is the total cost for Lindsay's dad and *x* is the number of gallons of regular gasoline purchased. For the Extend, students should be able to find the solution in a number of ways. The total cost in cents for Lindsay's dad will be $123x + 200$, where *x* is the number of gallons of regular gasoline purchased.

ACTIVITY 1-11 (p. 28)   GRAPHING LINEAR RELATIONSHIPS

Graphing the Cost Pattern for Gasoline and Oil

The activity is largely designed to help students create a TI-80 graph using the graph's defining relationship. Students will also use features of the TI-80 to explore the slope and *y*-intercept and their interpretations. They should discover that an increase of 1 gallon always produces a cost increase of \$1.23, indicating a constant rate of change. The number 1.23 is reflected as the coefficient in the equation for the total price, $y = 2 + 1.23x$. For the Extend, $Y2 = 4 + 1.43x$, where Y2 is the cost and *x* is the number of gallons of premium gasoline purchased. Students should be able to predict that the Extend graph will be steeper (slope of 1.43 rather than 1.23) and will have a greater *y*-intercept (4 rather than 2). They can easily check this prediction by drawing the graphs for Y1 and Y2 simultaneously on the TI-80.

ACTIVITY 1-12 (p. 29)   RATE OF CHANGE AND SLOPE

Patterns for Four Types of Gasoline

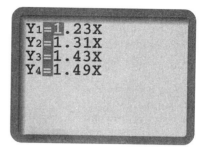

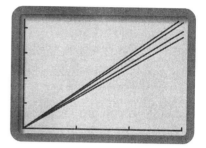

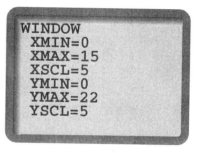

The key connection for this activity is that different gasoline costs, actually cost rates, translate into different slopes. Students will first need to consider the relationship between the total cost and the number of gallons purchased for various types of gasoline. Having generated the graphs, they will be in a position to find the slopes and make the connection between cost rate and slope. This should lead to the generalization that the higher the cost per gallon, the steeper the straight line representing total cost and number of gallons purchased.

The table and graph for the Extend are provided here. Notice that the slope is constant from $x = 0$ to $x = 5$, then becomes very slightly steeper from $x = 5$ to $x = 11$, and finally becomes very slightly steeper again from $x = 11$ to $x = 15$. The changes in slope are extremely small and therefore hardly recognizable on a graph.

Bill Blender's Purchase

Gallons of Gasoline	Total Cost
1	$1.23
2	2.46
3	3.69
4	4.92
5	6.15
6	7.46
7	8.77
8	10.08
9	11.39
10	12.70
11	14.01
12	15.44
13	16.87
14	18.30
15	19.73

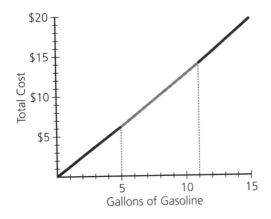

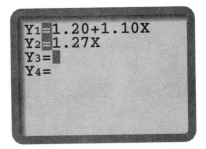

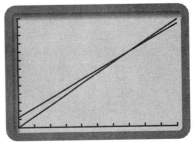

ACTIVITY 1-13 (p. 30) LINEAR RELATIONSHIPS

When Does Gerda Catch Peter?

This is a nice example of how graphical methods can be effectively used to solve a problem that will later be solved analytically. A complete table as well as equations and their corresponding TI-80 graphs follow.

Total Costs

Gallons of Gasoline	Peter's cost	Gerda's Cost
0	$1.75	$ 0
1	2.98	1.43
2	4.21	2.86
3	5.44	4.29
4	6.67	5.72
5	7.90	7.15
6	9.13	8.58
7	10.36	10.01
8	11.59	11.44
9	12.82	12.87
10	14.05	14.30

The costs are the same after both have pumped 8.75 gallons, and at that point the total cost for each is about $12.51. It will be important to have students justify why the intersection of the two lines is the point where the costs are the same. Connecting the table and the graph will help in stating such a justification. Teachers might ask students to talk more generally about the intersection of two lines and the interpretation of the coordinates of the intersection point. Questions such as "Do two lines always intersect?" and "Can two lines intersect at more than one point?" are useful for further explorations.

In the Extend, the straight line for Gerda, relating total cost and gallons purchased, is much steeper than her original one and hence the intersection point will occur more quickly. Actually, it occurs when the number of gallons pumped is about 6.73 and the total cost about $10.03.

ACTIVITY 1-14 (p. 31) LINEAR RELATIONSHIPS

Using the Two-Seat Ski Lift

Activity 1-14 begins a series of problems designed to introduce students to algebraic reasoning using symbols. It is important to help them explore the problems and discern relationships for themselves. This first problem follows an approach that has been developed in the earlier activities, so students should have little difficulty in determining that the number of people on the ski lift is $2r$ when r rows are filled. In the Extend, the total number of people on the ski lift is $2r + 6$. Students can show and justify their thinking with drawings or even algebra tiles, if they are available.

Graphing the Two-Seat Ski Lift

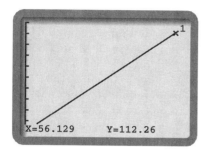

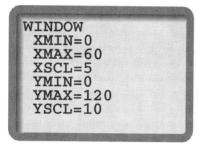

The first part of this problem is largely review, so you may want to use it as an assessment item. It also revisits the concepts of dependent and independent variables, as these need to be regularly reviewed. We also introduce informally the notion of *function*, a relationship in which there is exactly one value of the dependent variable for any given value of the independent variable. You may want to develop some additional problems and experiences to build students' understanding of function. The slope is 2 and an equation to represent the relationship is $y = 2x$. The constant slope of 2 indicates two additional people for each row on the lift. Also, there are 112 people on the lift when 56 rows are fully filled. The screen here shows the TRACE solution, approximately 112 people for 56 rows. In the Extend, we move from a functional relationship to a particular equation based on that function. The emphasis should be on generating the equation and solving it by largely informal means. For example, students could use guess and check, a graphing approach with TRACE, or reasoning based on inverse operations. When 48 people are on board the ski lift, 24 rows are filled; with 64 people, 32 rows are filled.

Simplifying Expressions

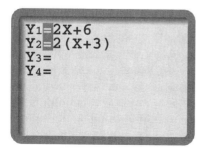

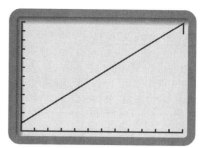

In this activity, students experience the development of equivalent algebraic expressions. Three criteria are considered for justifying equivalence: both expressions model the same situation; the corresponding functions generate the same tables; and the corresponding functions produce the same graph. The four screens show the two equations, the single graph, and the two tables, one for Y1 and one for Y2. Note that the y-values for a given x are identical. Also the vertical line in the upper right corner of the graph shows that the calculator is still plotting Y2, but nothing new is seen because Y1 and Y2 are equivalent. In the Extend, Francine's thinking is intended to show the symbolic process that transforms one expression into the other. She really justifies the existence of the distributive property. Students need to experience the kind of development inherent in this activity again and again, especially for key equivalencies like the distributive property.

Did Max Simplify the Expressions?

This activity is a valuable follow-up to the previous one. Using the same setting, an alternative and invalid algebraic equivalence is conjectured, and students have to investigate it and explain why it is not valid. Again, the table and graphing tools of the TI-80 can be used to compare the new conjecture to the original expression. Appropriate screens are shown here.

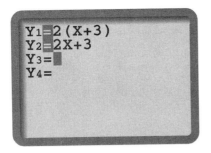

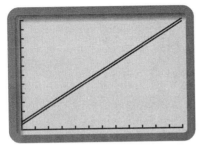

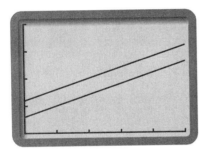

X	Y1
0	6
1	8
2	10
3	12
4	14
5	16

X=0

X	Y2
0	3
1	5
2	7
3	9
4	11
5	13

Y2=3

In the Extend, students are encouraged to write problems to show that $2(x - 1) = 2x - 2$. A sample is: The last row of each two-seat ski lift at Eagles' Nest Resort is left empty for safety reasons. If there are x rows on the two-seat lift, and all the others are filled, write down the number of people on the ski lift in two ways.

ACTIVITY 1-18 (p. 35)   EQUIVALENT EXPRESSIONS

Mixed Rows on the Three-Seat Ski Lift

The process developed in this activity is the same as that used earlier. However, the problem involves using the same variable twice in an expression. Again, we suggest that students be encouraged to write about what they are doing as a means of helping them to generalize the situation. When r rows of each category (two-seat and three-seat) are filled, the total number of skiers on board will be $2r + 3r$. Once again, Pam's thinking and the TI-80 can be used to help students recognize that $2r + 3r$ can be transformed into $5r$ or, alternatively, that these expressions are equivalent.

For the Extend, students need to define a variable, for instance, "Let r be the number of rows with three people." They then need to engage in some further algebraic modeling. Two equivalent expressions can be generated for the number of people on the ski lift, leading to the equation $3r + 2(r - 1) + 6 = 104$. It is hoped that a number of students will be able to simplify this equation to $3r + 2r - 2 + 6 = 104$ and on to $5r + 4 = 104$. Further simplification will be a bonus, but students should be able to solve the problem from here in a number of ways. The solution is $r = 20$; that is, the number of rows fully filled on the three-seat ski lift is 20. You might want to write problems similar to this to help students develop this kind of modeling.

Valentine's Day Fund Raiser

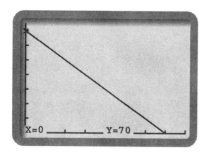

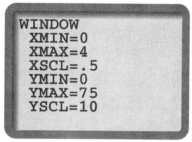

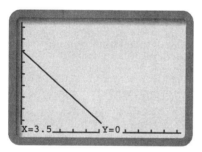

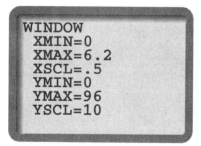

This is the first of a series of tasks that introduce non-linear relationships. The process for developing students' algebraic thinking is the same as before, and we commence by having students look for patterns in the table. They should note that the number of buyers decreases at a constant rate for each 20-cent increase in selling price, so this relationship is linear. The rate of

decrease is actually $\dfrac{4}{0.20}$ = 20 buyers per dollar, and

the relationship is $n = 70 - 20x$. If students are unable to determine this equation, provide it for them and have them check that it is a valid one. The Extend develops the graph of the relationship and enables the class to further discuss the negative slope and the intercepts. In the Extend, the x-axis intercept is needed. The graph shows a TRACE solution of $3.50 resulting in 0 buyers.

How Much Profit?

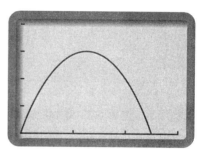

The problem in this activity is pivotal in building the non-linear relationship to describe profit. Students will again need to work through specific examples, make a table, and record what they are doing before trying to generalize. From the previous activity, $n = 70 - 20x$, where n is the number of buyers and x is the selling price in dollars. Because the cost of each card is $1, the profit on one card selling for x dollars is $x - 1$ dollars. Thus, the total profit when n buyers each purchase a card will be $n(x - 1) = (70 - 20x)(x - 1)$. An equivalent result can be found by realizing that the total selling price when n buyers purchase a card is
$nx = (70 - 20x)x$. The buying price of n cards is
n dollars = $(70 - 20x)$ dollars. The profit, in dollars, is then $(70 - 20x)x - (70 - 20x)$ which can factored using the common factor $(70 - 20x)$ to be $(70 - 20x)(x - 1)$. Even if students can't factor the second profit expression, they could show that the two expressions are equivalent by comparing their graphs on the TI-80.

For the Extend, the profit is $p = \dfrac{(70 - 0.2x)(x - 100)}{100}$,

where x is the selling price in cents.

ACTIVITY 1-21 (p. 38)　　　QUADRATIC RELATIONSHIPS

Graphing the Profit

In this activity, students will explore the graph of the non-linear relationship found in Activity 1-20. The relationship is quadratic, and the graph is a parabola. The technology will be especially helpful in noting that the profit increases up to a maximum of approximately $31.25 and then decreases. Use of TRACE will also enable students to see that the profit is zero when the selling price is $1 and that the profit is again zero when the selling price is $3.50. For the extension, TRACE can be used to show that when the selling price is $2 the profit is $30. This profit occurs again when the selling price is approximately $2.50.

ACTIVITY 1-22 (p. 39)　　　RATES OF CHANGE

Does the Profit Change at a Constant Rate?

This task provides a good opportunity for students to examine the rate of change for the profit function and to contrast it with the rate of change of the buyers' function. In the case of the buyers-per-day function, there are 4 fewer buyers for every 20 cent increase. This means that there are 20 fewer buyers per dollar increase in the selling price. Carla's question about the profit function is appropriate, because the rate of change for the profit function is not constant. The table shown with the notes for Activity 1-20 verifies this. To create this table on the TI-80, press 2_{nd} TblSet and input a minimum of 1 and an increment of 0.2. Display the table with 2_{nd} TblSet and show that the profit change from $x = 1$ to $x = 2$ increases by 30, yet from $x = 2$ to $x = 3$ (arrow down in the table) it decreases by 10. This is clearly not constant either numerically or in direction. For the extension, the profit is increasing most quickly between $x = 1$ and $x = 1.4$ and is decreasing most quickly between $x = 3$ and $x = 3.4$. The profit is hardly changing between $x = 2$ and $x = 2.4$. Answers will vary depending on students' table settings, that is, their starting values and increments.

Applying Activities

ACTIVITY 1-23 (p. 40)　　　LINEAR RELATIONSHIPS

The Lemonade Stand

X	Y1
0	0
5	60
10	120
15	180
20	240
25	300
X=0	

The first three Applying activities deal with linear relationships. This activity could be used as a focus for review or as an assessment task. For the first part of the activity, $P = 15x - 3x$, where P is the profit in cents and x is the number of glasses sold. Students should be able to solve this problem in at least two ways (see Activity 1-24), and should also be able to transform it to $P = 12x$. For the Extend, $P = 12x - 25(3) = 12x - 75$, because 25 glasses are produced but are not sold.

ACTIVITY 1-24 (p. 41)　　　EQUIVALENT EXPRESSIONS

Finding the Lemonade-Stand Profit

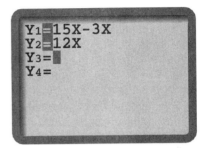

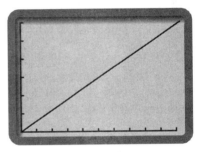

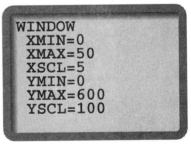

This activity makes more explicit the two solutions suggested in the notes for Activity 1-23. Lynn's profit function is $P = 15x - 3x$ and Teiko's is $P = 12x$. Students using methods outlined earlier (Activity 1-16) should justify why the profit functions are equivalent. For the Extend, students could enter two functions, $Y1 = 15x - 2.5x$ and $Y2 = 12.5x$, into the TI-80 and graph them. The graphs of these functions are identical, showing that they are equivalent.

ACTIVITY 1-25 (p. 42)   EQUIVALENT EXPRESSIONS

Economy Class

This activity focuses on algebraic modeling and using algebraic reasoning to solve equations and to show that expressions are equivalent. If the class has covered all the Developing activities, this task could be used as an assessment problem. If there are r rows in the middle, the number of seats in the economy cabin is $5r + 2(r - 1) + 2(r - 1)$. Using different reasoning, the number of seats could also be formulated as $5r + 2r - 2 + 2r - 2$. In the latter case, students simply take one row consisting of two seats from each side of the cabin. Both of these expressions can be transformed into $9r - 4$, or students could develop this expression from the original problem setting. In the Extend, one solution would be to argue that $9r - 4 = 239$ and then show that $r = 27$.

ACTIVITY 1-26 (p. 43)   QUADRATIC RELATIONSHIPS

A Bowling Tournament

This activity deals with a quadratic relationship and could be used either as a review or as an assessment. Students should be able to express the general relationship from some special cases or from a table. If n is the number of games played and x is the number of girls who register for the tournament, $n = \dfrac{x(x - 1)}{2}$.

You might want to probe students as to why the expression $x(x - 1)$ must be divided by 2. The Extend can be solved in a number of ways. One solution can be produced by graphing $Y1 = \dfrac{x(x - 1)}{2}$, setting an appropriate window, and using TRACE to locate any x-values when Y1 is 990. This process will generate a solution close to 45. Another solution can be determined by arguing that $x(x - 1) = 2(990) = 1980$. A guess-and-check strategy or taking approximations using the square root of 1980 as a guide will reveal that $x = 45$.

ACTIVITY 1-27 (p. 44)   EXPONENTIAL RELATIONSHIPS

Brent's Savings Plan

The next two activities introduce an exponential function. While the equation of the function and its properties are different from linear and quadratic functions, the process of exploring exponential functions is the same as we have used previously. In other words, the algebraic reasoning is similar, but the characteristics of exponential functions are different. In this task,

students could be encouraged to look at special cases, to make a table, to draw a graph, and to look for patterns within and between variables. If d is the number of dollars put into his account at the beginning of week x, then $d = 2^{x - 1}$. In this relationship, the value of d is always double its value the previous week; so we call 2 the *growth factor* or *growth rate* for the relationship. Notice that the growth factor, 2, is also the base in the exponential function. The contrast with the linear function $y = 2x$ provides a valuable exploration for students. In the case of the linear function, y increases 2 units for every unit change in x. However, for the exponential function, $d = 2^{x - 1}$, d is doubled for every unit change in x.

For the Extend, students could find several answers. One answer is: $t = 1 + 2^1 + 2^2 + \ldots + 2^{x - 1}$, where t is the cumulative amount in Brent's savings account after x weeks. This is found by adding the amounts deposited each week. A second solution can be obtained by making a table listing the cumulative amounts in Brent's account each week. The pattern in this table leads to the relationship $t = 2^x - 1$.

ACTIVITY 1-28 (p. 45)   EXPONENTIAL RELATIONSHIPS

Graphing Brent's Savings Plan

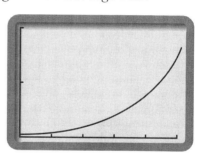

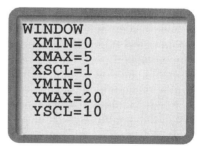

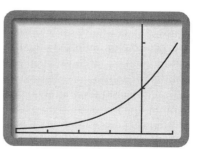

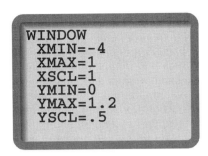

This task focuses on the characteristics and properties of the graph of the exponential function $d = 2^{x-1}$. The properties include the following: values of d are always positive even for negative values of x, the graph passes through the y-axis at the point $\left(0, \frac{1}{2}\right)$, the graph does not pass through the x-axis but approaches it closely when x takes large negative values, values of d increase very rapidly for positive values of x, and the graph does not grow at a constant rate.

For the Extend, if w is the amount withdrawn at the beginning of week x, then

$$w = \frac{1}{5}\left[500\left(\frac{4}{5}\right)^{x-1}\right] = 100\left(\frac{4}{5}\right)^{x-1}.$$ In this case the growth fact is $\frac{4}{5}$, but it is really a decay factor in that each value of w is $\frac{4}{5}$ its value the previous week.

Challenging Activities

ACTIVITY 1-29 (p. 46)   QUADRATIC RELATIONSHIPS

Softball Fallout

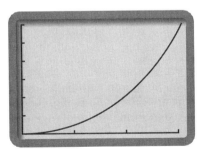

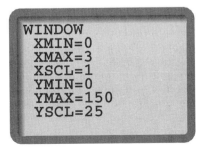

This task could be a valuable assessment project. You may even want students to collect their own data. For the data given, the relationship between y and t is $y = 16t^2$. Students may recognize this as a quadratic function with the shape of a parabola. A graph constructed with the TI-80 will confirm this, although the relationship is plotted for only positive values of t.

The Extend could be solved in a number of ways. One relatively simple solution is to find the average velocity for any period of time. For example, because the ball drops 100 feet in 2.5 seconds, the average speed is

$$\frac{100}{2.5} = 40 \text{ ft/sec. In considering the drop from 100 feet,}$$

a better approximation of its speed near the ground can be obtained by using the fact that it takes 2 seconds to drop the first 64 feet from rest (zero speed). This means that it takes 0.5 seconds to travel the last

36 feet and hence averages $\frac{36}{0.5} = 72$ ft/sec over this

distance. This will be closer to its maximum speed of 80 ft/sec, which occurs just as it hits the ground.

ACTIVITY 1-30 (p. 47)   EXPONENTIAL RELATIONSHIPS

Fruit Juice and Cookies

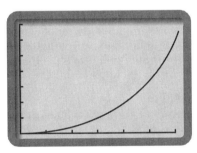

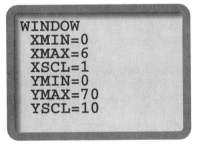

You may wish to use this activity as an assessment project, having students work in groups. They could look at special cases, make a table, draw a graph, and look for different patterns. If f is the number of friends invited for fruit juice and cookies on the nth day, then $f = 2^n$. The shape of the graph of this relationship is exponential, with properties similar to those listed in Activity 1-28. For the Extend, the total amount of money raised after n days is given by t, where $t = (2^{n+1} - 2)(0.25)$.

Bouncing a Tennis Ball

In 2 minutes, how many times can you bounce and catch a tennis ball, each time dropping it from your waist?

Investigate

Predict the total number of bounces you can make in 2 minutes, and then carry out the experiment as a group. One person keeps the time, another person bounces and catches the ball, and a third person counts the bounces. A fourth person can record the data in a table showing the total number of bounces—the cumulative total—after each 10-second period of a 2-minute experiment.

Share

Examine your table. Describe any patterns you see in the number of bounces.

Describe any pattern you see between the number of seconds elapsed and the number of bounces.

Extend

Use your results to predict how many times you could bounce and catch the tennis ball in 4 minutes. What factors might influence your prediction?

DEVELOPING
ACTIVITY 1-2

Graphing the Tennis-Ball Bounces

Data Set 1: Tennis-Ball-Bounce Data gives data similar to the data you may have collected in Activity 1-1: Bouncing a Tennis Ball. How can you use the TI-80 to display a visual relationship between the total number of bounces and the times shown in Data Set 1?

Investigate

Enter into list L1 of your calculator the 10-second time values between 0 and 120 seconds. Enter into list L2 of your calculator the total number of bounces for each time shown in Data Set 1. Use Calculator Help 1: Entering Lists and Calculator Help 6: Scatter Plot to construct the plot.

- Set the window using appropriate values for the horizontal and vertical axes.
- Define and display the scatter plot according to the steps described in the calculator help.

Your screen should look like the one shown here.

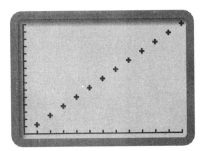

Share

What do you notice about the pattern of points on the scatter plot? Write a short paragraph to describe the pattern you see. Share it with your classmates. Did you all see the same pattern?

Look back at Data Set 1. Examine any patterns you see in the cumulative number of bounces. How is this pattern revealed in the scatter plot?

Now look in Data Set 1 for patterns between the number of seconds elapsed and the cumulative number of bounces. Is this pattern revealed in the scatter plot? Explain.

Extend

Colleen was ill the day her class collected the tennis-ball-bounce data. Her mother helped her carry out the experiment and collect the data shown in Data Set 2. Do Colleen's data really reveal different patterns from those you found for Data Set 1? Explain.

DEVELOPING
ACTIVITY 1-3

Growth in the Number of Bounces

Using the tennis-ball-bounce data in Data Set 1, what is the rate of tennis-ball bounces per second?

Investigate

Examine the table or the scatter plot from Activity 1-2: Graphing the Tennis-Ball Bounces. By how many bounces does the number of tennis-ball bounces increase in each 20-second interval? How can you use this information to solve the problem?

Share

What is the rate of tennis-ball bounces per second? Describe how you determined this rate, both from the table in Data Set 1 and from the scatter plot.

This rate is called the *slope of the line* revealed in your scatter plot, here expressed in bounces per second. Marion suggested that her scatter plot showed a constant slope. What do you suppose she meant by that?

Extend

Lindsay asked her grandfather to carry out the tennis-ball-bounce experiment. The scatter plot showing the relationship between the total number of bounces and time in seconds for her grandfather is shown here. How can you describe the slope in this case? Is the slope constant? Explain your thinking.

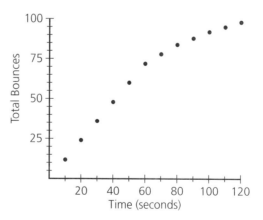

Packing the Tennis Balls

In her part-time job, Kim packs tennis balls into square boxes as shown in the diagram. How many tennis balls will she pack into square boxes that are 1 tennis ball high and have side lengths that range from 1 tennis-ball unit to 20 tennis-ball units?

Investigate

Draw appropriate diagrams and construct a table to show the number of tennis balls in a square box as the side length of the box increases from 1 tennis-ball unit to 20 tennis-ball units.

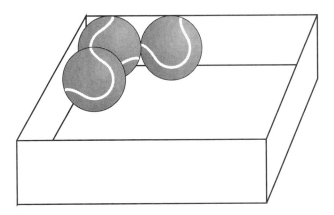

Share

What quantities vary in this problem?

Examine your table. Do you see any pattern in the number of tennis balls per box as the box size increases? Describe any patterns you see.

Can you see any pattern or relationship between the side length of the box in tennis-ball units and the number of balls the box will hold? If so, describe the pattern.

Extend

Predict the number of tennis balls that would fit in a super-sized square box whose side length is 40 tennis-ball units. Explain the basis for your prediction.

Graphing the Tennis-Ball-Packing Data

How can you use the TI-80 with the data from Activity 1-4: Packing the Tennis Balls to determine a visual relationship between the total number of tennis balls in a square box with height one tennis-ball unit and the length of the side of the box in tennis-ball units?

Investigate

Enter into list L1 of your calculator the side lengths in tennis-ball units, ranging from 0 to 20. Enter into list L2 of your calculator the total number of tennis balls in the box for each side length. Use Calculator Help 6: Scatter Plot to construct the plot.

- Set the window using appropriate values for the horizontal and vertical axes.
- Define and display the scatter plot according to the steps described in the calculator help.

Share

What do you notice about the pattern of points on the scatter plot? Write a short paragraph to describe the pattern you see and share it with your classmates. Did you all see the same pattern?

Look for patterns between the side length in tennis-ball units and the total number of tennis balls in the box for each side length. Describe any pattern you see and indicate how it is revealed in the scatter plot.

Extend

Is there a visual relationship between the number of tennis balls in a square box and the length of the side of the box in inches? Explain your thinking and construct a graph for this new relationship. How does your new scatter plot compare to your first scatter plot?

DEVELOPING
ACTIVITY 1-6

Growth in the Number of Tennis Balls

Use the tennis-ball-packing data from Activity 1-4 or the graphical display from Activity 1-5 to find the rate at which the total number of tennis balls is changing per unit increase in the side length of the box, where one unit is one tennis ball. Is this rate constant? Why or why not?

Investigate

Examine the table or the scatter plot. What is the increase in the total number of tennis balls in the box for each unit increase in the side length of the box? Complete the table to record your thinking.

Rate of Change

Increase in Side Length of Box	Change in Number of Tennis Balls in Box
from: 0 to 1 units	?
1 to 2	?
2 to 3	5 tennis balls
3 to 4	?
.	.
.	.
.	.

How can you use this information to solve the problem?

Share

What can you say about the rate of change in the total number of tennis balls in the box per unit increase in the side length? Is the rate of change constant? Is the rate in this problem different from the rate you investigated in Growth in the Number of Tennis-Ball Bounces (Activity 1-3)? Explain.

Extend

Does it make sense to determine the rate of increase in the total number of tennis balls in the box for each one-inch increase in the side length of the box? Explain.

Buying Regular Gasoline

Bev's dad buys regular unleaded gasoline that is advertised for $1.23 per gallon at the local filling station. How much will it cost Bev's dad to buy 5 gallons of regular gasoline? How much will it cost for 20 gallons? Find a way to determine the cost when various numbers of gallons are purchased.

Investigate

Work in pairs to construct both a table and a scatter plot to explore the problem.

Share

How can you use your table or your scatter plot to determine the cost for various amounts of gasoline? Write a short paragraph to describe your method and then share it with your classmates.

Explain other ways to determine the cost for various amounts of gasoline.

Extend

Before going on a long trip, Bev's dad purchases regular-plus unleaded gasoline that is advertised for $1.31 per gallon at the local filling station. If he puts 15 gallons in his tank, how much more will he pay for regular plus than if he had used the same amount of regular gasoline?

DEVELOPING
ACTIVITY 1-8

A Cost Pattern for Regular Gasoline

> Use your exploration of Activity 1-7: Buying Regular Gasoline to describe a pattern that enables you to find the cost of regular gasoline no matter how many gallons are purchased. Describe your pattern by finding the cost when Bev's dad purchases *g* gallons of regular gasoline.

Investigate
Look at your table in Activity 1-7. How did you find the cost for 1 gallon of gasoline? For 2 gallons? For 5 gallons? For *g* gallons?

Share
Why was it helpful to look at your table when trying to find the cost of regular gasoline when various amounts are purchased?

What is the cost of purchasing *g* gallons of regular gasoline? Explain your thinking.

Extend
Here's a problem that Sylvia began to solve.

Bev's dad found an old receipt in his car. It showed that he spent $16.20 on regular gasoline when the price was $1.08 per gallon. How many gallons did he purchase?

Sylvia said, "The cost of purchasing *g* gallons of the gasoline is $1.08*g*. This means that $1.08g = 16.20$."

Is Sylvia's reasoning correct? Why or why not? If her reasoning is correct, use it to complete the solution to the problem. If it is not correct, find another way to solve the problem.

Regular Gasoline and Motor Oil

Lindsay's dad also buys regular unleaded gasoline that costs $1.23 per gallon, but every time he purchases gasoline he also purchases a quart of motor oil that costs $2. What is the total cost for gasoline and motor oil for Lindsay's dad when he purchases 5 gallons of regular gasoline? What is the total cost when he purchases 20 gallons? Find a way to determine the total cost for gasoline and motor oil when Lindsay's dad purchases various amounts of gasoline.

Investigate Work in pairs to construct both a table and a scatter plot to explore the problem.

Share How can you use your table or your scatter plot to determine the cost for gasoline and motor oil for various amounts of gasoline? Write a short paragraph to describe your method and then share it with your classmates.

Describe at least one other way to determine the cost for various amounts of gasoline.

What does your table or scatter plot tell you about the total cost for gasoline and motor oil when Lindsay's dad buys 0 gallons of gasoline? Interpret this within the context of the problem.

Extend Before going on a long trip, Lindsay's dad purchases super unleaded gasoline that costs $1.48 per gallon at the local filling station as well as his usual quart of motor oil for $2. How much more will his total bill be if he buys 15 gallons of super gasoline than if he buys the same quantity of regular gasoline? Try to solve the problem in more than one way.

DEVELOPING
ACTIVITY 1-10

A Cost Pattern for Gasoline and Oil

Use your exploration from Activity 1-9: Regular Gasoline and Motor Oil to describe a pattern that will enable you to find the total cost for Lindsay's dad no matter how many gallons of regular gas he purchases. Describe your pattern by finding the total cost when Lindsay's dad purchases *x* gallons of regular gasoline.

Investigate   Look at your table in Activity 1-9. How did you find the total cost of gasoline and motor oil for 1 gallon of gasoline? For 2 gallons? For 5 gallons? For *x* gallons?

Share   How did you determine the total cost for gasoline and motor oil for various amounts of gasoline? Was it more helpful to look at the relationships between amounts of gasoline and total costs or to look just at the total costs?

What was the total cost for gasoline and motor oil when purchasing *x* gallons of regular gasoline? Explain your thinking.

Extend   If you decide to work in cents rather than dollars, how will the pattern for total cost of gasoline and motor oil change? Illustrate your thinking by finding the total cost in cents for gasoline and motor oil when Lindsay's dad purchases *x* gallons of gasoline.

DEVELOPING
ACTIVITY 1-11

Graphing the Cost Pattern for Gasoline and Oil

> In Activity 1-10: A Cost Pattern for Gasoline and Motor Oil, Lotus found that the total cost for gasoline and motor oil for x gallons of gasoline was $2 + $1.23x. He knew how to graph this relationship on the TI-80 calculator. How did Lotus do it?

Investigate

Before using the calculator, Lotus wrote the following information in his notebook:

I'll let x represent the number of gallons of gasoline purchased and y represent the total cost in dollars. Since y depends on x and I have to include $2 for oil, I can write the equation $y = 2 + 1.23x$.

Use the Calculator Help 10: Graphing a Function to re-create the graph shown here.

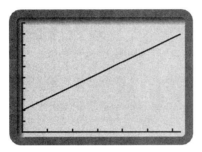

- Press [Y=] and enter Lotus's relationship.
- Press [WINDOW] and enter the same window Lotus used (0, 6.2, 1; 0, 10, 1).
- Press [GRAPH] to display the relationship between total cost and gallons purchased.

Share

Describe your calculator graph. What does the graph tell you when Lindsay's dad purchases 0 gallons of gasoline? How is this value represented in the equation? This value is called the y-intercept of the graph. Why is that an appropriate name?

Use the [TRACE] key to find the change in the total cost for gasoline and motor oil when the amount of gasoline purchased increases from 0 to 1 gallon, from 1 to 2 gallons, and from 2 to 3 gallons. What do you notice about these values? How is this related to the slope of the graph? How is it represented in the equation?

Extend

What would Lotus's equation be if Lindsay's dad paid $4 for motor oil and used premium unleaded gasoline that costs $1.43 per gallon? Use Y2 to represent the total cost of gasoline and motor oil and use x to represent the number of gallons of gasoline.

Without drawing the graph, describe how it would change from the one you just created.

DEVELOPING
ACTIVITY 1-12
Patterns for Four Types of Gasoline

Max's Garage offers four types of gasoline: regular for $1.23 per gallon; super for $1.31 per gallon; premium for $1.43 per gallon; and super plus for $1.49 per gallon. For each gasoline type, find an equation that describes the total cost when x gallons of gasoline are purchased. Draw the graphs and compare their slopes.

Investigate

Use Lotus's method from Activity 1-11 to find the equation for each gasoline type and to construct its graph. The purchase of motor oil is not part of this problem. Use the calculator variables Y1, Y2, Y3, and Y4, together with an appropriate window choice, to draw all four graphs on the same screen.

Share

How are the four graphs alike and how do they differ? In your description, be sure to use the terms slope and y-intercept.

Can you tell just by looking which graph represents the most expensive gasoline and which represents the least expensive? Explain your thinking.

Extend

Bill Blender has a distinctive approach when purchasing gasoline at Max's Garage. First he puts in 5 gallons of regular, then 6 gallons of super and finally 4 gallons of premium. Construct a table to show Bill's gasoline costs after 5 gallons, 11 gallons, and 15 gallons. Then use graph paper to construct an appropriate graph to show the cost for Bill's gasoline after various numbers of gallons have been pumped.

When you are finished, describe your graph and discuss its slope at various stages of the fill up.

DEVELOPING
ACTIVITY 1-13

When Does Gerda Catch Peter?

Peter owes Max $1.75 and asks him to include this amount with his purchase of 10 gallons of regular gasoline at $1.23 per gallon. At the same time, Gerda is filling her car with 10 gallons of premium gasoline at $1.43 per gallon. On the same axes, construct graphs for both Peter's total cost and Gerda's total cost when the amount of gasoline pumped varies from 0 to 10 gallons. Assume that Peter's total cost is $1.75 before he begins to pump any gasoline. Use your graphs to determine when the total costs for Peter and Gerda are the same.

Investigate

Use Lotus's method from Activity 1-11 to find the equations for both Peter's and Gerda's total gasoline costs.

Total Costs

Gallons of Gasoline	Peter's Cost	Gerda's Cost
0		
.		
.		
.		
10		

Create a table like the one here to show the total costs for Peter and Gerda for various amounts of gasoline.

Then use the TI-80 to construct the graphs for both Peter's total cost and Gerda's total cost when the amount of gasoline pumped varies from 0 to 10 gallons. Draw both graphs on the same screen.

Share

What does your table tell you about the total gasoline costs for Peter and Gerda as they fill their tanks? How do the total costs change, relative to each other, as they fill their tanks? When are their total costs the same? How did you determine that?

Do the two graphs give you the same information as the table? Explain your thinking. Could you use the graphs to find when their total costs are the same? If so, describe how.

Extend

Suppose Gerda had purchased 10 gallons of super-plus at $1.49 per gallon. Would she have reached the same total cost as Peter more quickly or less quickly than when she filled with premium? Justify your response.

DEVELOPING
ACTIVITY 1-14

Using the Two-Seat Ski Lift

> One of the ski lifts at Silver Snow Resort has two seats per row.
> How many people will be on the ski lift if 5, 15, 20, or 28 rows are
> fully filled? Find a way to determine the number of people on the
> ski lift when various numbers of rows are fully filled. Illustrate your
> approach by finding the number of people on the ski lift when r
> rows are fully filled.

Investigate   Work in pairs to find a pattern that will allow you to determine the number of
people on the ski lift when various numbers of rows are filled. Use this pattern to
determine the number of people on the ski lift when r rows are filled.

Share   Describe the pattern and indicate how you found that pattern.

What is the number of people on the ski lift when r rows are filled? Justify your
response.

Extend   Suppose the ski lift had r rows fully filled and 6 rows each with only one person on
board. How many people would be on the ski lift? Justify your solution and draw a
diagram to illustrate your thinking.

DEVELOPING
ACTIVITY 1-15 | Graphing the Two-Seat Ski Lift

Use your TI-80 to construct a graph that shows the relationship between the number of people on the two-seat ski lift and the number of rows fully filled. Use your graph to determine the number of people on the ski lift when 56 rows are fully filled.

Investigate

One variable in this problem is the number of fully filled rows on the two-seat ski lift. Let's represent that variable by x. The other variable in this problem is the total number of people on the ski lift, which depends on x. We will represent this total number of people by Y1. Because Y1 depends on x, we say that x is the *independent variable* and Y1 is the *dependent variable*. Because every x has exactly one Y1 value, we say that Y1 is a function of x. Write the equation for the relationship.

Use your equation and Calculator Help 10: Graphing a Function to create a graph of the function that describes the relationship between the number of people on the two-seat ski lift and the number of rows fully filled.

- Press Y= and enter your equation.
- Press WINDOW and enter an appropriate window.
- Press GRAPH to display the relationship between the number of fully filled rows and the number of people on the ski lift.

Share

Describe your graph. Indicate whether its slope is constant. How did you determine that? What is the slope? Interpret the slope within the original problem involving people on the ski lift.

Extend

Use your graph to determine the number of rows that are fully filled when 48 people are on the two-seat ski lift.

Tom solved this problem without using his graph. He said, "Suppose there are x rows. Then $2x = 48$ and hence $x = 24$."

What do you think about Tom's solution? How do you think he went from the equation $2x = 48$ to the solution $x = 24$?

Use Tom's method to determine the number of rows that are fully filled when 64 people are on the ski lift.

DEVELOPING
ACTIVITY 1-16 # Simplifying Expressions

> Irena and Goran solved the following problem in two ways.
>
> Suppose a two-seat ski lift had x rows fully filled and 6 rows each with only one person on board. How many people would be on the ski lift?
>
> Goran said, "There are x rows with two people in each row, so that's $2x$ people. Then we add on the other 6 people. This makes a total of $2x + 6$ people on the ski lift."
>
> Irena said, "There are 6 rows with only one person in each row. That's the same as having 3 fully filled two-seat rows. So the total number of rows is $x + 3$, and the total number of people on that two-seat lift is $2(x + 3)$."
>
> Are both solutions correct?

Investigate

Graph these two functions on your calculator, calling Goran's Y1 = $2x + 6$ and Irena's Y2 = $2(x + 3)$. What do you notice?

Use Calculator Help 11: Creating a Table to make a TI-80 table for both Goran's and Irena's functions (Y1 and Y2).

- Press Y= and be sure Y1 and Y2 are entered correctly.
- Press WINDOW and check for an appropriate window.
- Press 2nd TblSet and key in 0 for TBLMIN and 1 for ΔTBL.
- Press 2nd TABLE to display the table for Y1.
- Use ▶ to display the table for Y2.

What do you notice about the tables for Y1 and Y2?

Share

Are Irena's and Goran's solutions both correct? Why or why not? Share your thinking with the class.

Was there one graph or were there two graphs? Explain.

What do the tables and graphs you have created tell you about the two solutions?

Extend

Francine says, "I would have predicted that the two solutions are the same. Look. If we multiply out Irena's solution, $2(x + 3)$, we get 2 times x plus 2 times 3, or just $2(x) + 2(3)$. But this is the same as $2x + 6$, which is Goran's solution. They're equivalent!"

Is Francine correct? How do you know?

Did Max Simplify the Expression?

In solving the Extend to Activity 1-16: Simplifying Expressions, Max disagreed with Francine's solution. He said, "I think that $2(x + 3)$ should be equal to $2x + 3$."

Is Max correct? How do you know?

Investigate

Use the table and graphing tools of the TI-80 to investigate Max's conjecture.

Share

What did you find in your investigation of Max's conjecture? Share your findings with the class.

Extend

Write $2(x - 1)$ in an equivalent form. How can you check to be sure you are correct?

Make up a story using the two-seat ski-lift setting to show that $2(x - 1)$ and its equivalent form are the same.

DEVELOPING
ACTIVITY 1-18

Mixed Rows on the Three-Seat Ski Lift

During ski-instruction periods, the three-seat ski lift has some rows of seats fully filled and some rows with only two people. If the number of rows with three people is the same as the number of rows with two people, how many people will be on the ski lift if 5 rows have three people and another 5 rows have only two people? What about 15, 20, 25, and 30 rows of each category?

Vary the number of rows and find a way to determine the number of skiers on the ski lift when the same number of rows of each category are present. Illustrate your thinking by finding the number of skiers on the ski lift when *r* rows of each category are filled.

Investigate

Work in pairs to find a pattern that will allow you to determine the number of people on the ski lift when various numbers of rows of each category (two-seat and three-seat) are filled. Use this pattern to determine the number of people on the ski lift when *r* rows of each category are filled.

Share

Describe your pattern and explain how you found the number of skiers on the lift when *r* rows of each category are filled.

Pam says, "The number of skiers on the lift when *r* rows of each category are filled is *5r*. This is because $2r + 3r$ is the same as $5r$." Is Pam correct? Justify your response. Does it help to use the TI-80 to plot the graphs of $Y1 = 2x + 3x$ and $Y2 = 5x$? Explain.

Extend

On the last run of the day, the ski lift has a certain number of rows with three people. The number of rows with two people is one less than the number of rows with three people. Finally, there are 6 rows with only one person on board. If there are 104 people on the ski lift, how many rows are fully filled?

Valentine's Day Fund Raiser

The sixth-grade class at Boomerang Middle School is selling valentines to raise money for recreation equipment for the school. The cost of each card to the sixth-grade class is $1. The students have discovered that when they vary the selling price of their cards, the number of buyers per day changes. The table below shows what they have found.

Valentine-Buying Patterns

Selling Price ($)	1.00	1.20	1.40	1.60	1.80	2.00	2.20
Buyers per Day	50	46	42	38	34	30	26

Find a way to determine the number of buyers per day when various selling prices are used. If we use n to represent the number of buyers per day when the selling price is x dollars, find a relationship between n and x.

Investigate

Work in pairs to find a pattern that will allow you to determine the number of buyers per day when various selling prices are used. Use your pattern to determine the number of buyers, n, when the selling price is x dollars.

Share

Describe your pattern and explain how you found the number of buyers n when the selling price is x dollars per card.

Does the number of buyers increase at a constant rate for each dollar increase in the selling price? Explain your thinking and predict what the graph of this relationship will look like.

Extend

Use the TI-80 to construct a graph showing the relationship between the number of buyers per day and a card's selling price. From the graph determine the selling price that will result in 0 buyers per day. Explain what this result means.

DEVELOPING
ACTIVITY 1-20

How Much Profit?

Referring to the data in Activity 1-19: Valentine's Day Fund Raiser, Doug says, "I wonder how our profit will change when we vary the selling price?" Respond to Doug's question by determining the profit in dollars when various selling prices are used. If the selling price is x dollars, find the total profit p in dollars.

Investigate

A table has been started to show the number of buyers and the total profit for a variety of selling prices. In calculating the total profit, it is important to remember that the cost of each card is $1, and therefore the profit on a card selling for $1.20 is $0.20. How was the total profit of $9.20 calculated for the table entry shown here?

Determining Profit

Selling Price	Number of Buyers	Total Profit
$1.20	46	$9.20

Complete the table for several more selling prices and then find the total profit when the selling price is x dollars.

Share

Write a paragraph to describe a process by which you can determine the total profit when you know the selling price for a card. Can you use the process to determine a relationship between the total profit p and the selling price per card x?

In finding the total profit, when the selling price is x dollars, John said, "The profit on each card is $x - 1$ dollars and the number of card buyers is $70 - 20x$. This tells me that the total profit is the product of these two expressions, that is, $(x - 1)(70 - 20x)$." Is John's reasoning correct? Why or why not? Where did John get $70 - 20x$?

Extend

Kim says, "I have a question. Suppose the selling price had been listed in cents rather than dollars. What is the profit in dollars if the selling price was x cents?" Respond to the question raised by Kim. Explain and illustrate your thinking.

DEVELOPING
ACTIVITY 1-21

Graphing the Profit

Use your TI-80 calculator to construct a graph to show the relationship between the selling price in dollars and the total profit in dollars for the Valentine's Day fund raiser. What does the graph tell you about the total profit for various selling prices? What can the sixth-grade class do to maximize their profit?

Investigate

Before using the calculator, Judy wrote the following information in her notebook:

I'll let x represent the selling price per card in dollars and y represent the total profit in dollars. I know from the previous activity that the equation $y = (x - 1)(70 - 20x)$ expresses the relationship between x and y.

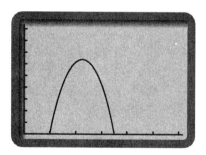

Use Calculator Help 10: Graphing a Function to re-create the graph shown here.

- Press [Y=] and enter Judy's relationship.
- Press [WINDOW] and enter the same window Judy used (0, 6.2, 1; 0, 48, 5).
- Press [GRAPH] to display the relationship between total profit and selling price per card.

Share

Describe the graph you have drawn with your calculator. What does the graph tell you about the total profit for various selling prices per card? What selling price produces a maximum profit for the sixth-grade class? What is that maximum profit? Explain how you determined these values.

What does the graph tell you about the total profit when the selling price is $1? Why would you have expected this? Does a similar total profit situation occur again? At what selling price? Why does this occur again?

Extend

Ella Mae said, "I used the [TRACE] key on the graph and it told me that when the selling price is $2 the total profit is $30." Find the other selling price that Ella Mae could have found that results in a total profit of $30. Explain how you determined this second selling price.

DEVELOPING
ACTIVITY 1-22

Does the Profit Change at a Constant Rate?

Carla says, "When we were doing the Valentine's Day fund raiser activity, we found a constant change in the number of buyers per $1 increase in the selling price. I thought that would cause the profit to also change at a constant rate for every $1 increase in the selling price. Now that I've looked at the total profit graph, I'm not sure." How can you respond to Carla's dilemma?

Investigate   Use the graph and table features of the TI-80 calculator to explore Carla's dilemma.

Share   Was the total profit changing at a constant rate for every $1 increase in the selling price? Write a report to explain and justify your response.

Extend   Use your table or your graph to determine when the profit is increasing most quickly, when it is decreasing most quickly, and when it is hardly changing.

APPLYING
ACTIVITY 1-23

The Lemonade Stand

> Amy and Malik set up a lemonade stand during the summer. If each glass of lemonade costs 3 cents to produce and they sell each glass for 15 cents, find a way to determine the profit when various numbers of glasses of lemonade are sold. If p is the profit, in cents, and x is the number of glasses sold, find an equation that relates p and x.

Investigate

How can you construct a table to relate the amount of profit to various numbers of glasses sold?

What pattern is there in the way that you determined the profit for various numbers of glasses sold?

Share

Write an explanation to describe how you determined the profit for various numbers of glasses of lemonade sold. How did your explanation help you find an equation that relates p and x?

Write the equation that relates the profit p to the number of glasses of lemonade sold x.

Extend

Suppose there are 25 glasses of lemonade left over at the end of the day. How would that affect the profit? Explain your thinking and write a relationship to show how the profit would be affected if x glasses were sold.

APPLYING
ACTIVITY 1-24

Finding the Lemonade-Stand Profit

> Lynn and Teiko used two different approaches to find the profit when x glasses of lemonade were sold in Activity 1-23: The Lemonade Stand.
>
> Lynn said, "The income when x glasses are sold is $15x$, and the cost of producing the lemonade is $3x$. The profit will be. . . ."
>
> Teiko said, "The profit on each glass of lemonade is 12 cents. So the profit on x glasses will be. . . ."
>
> First use Lynn's reasoning and then Teiko's to find the profit on x glasses. Are the two expressions for the profit the same?

Investigate

Write two equations for the profit, one using Lynn's reasoning and the other using Teiko's reasoning.

Use the TI-80 calculator to construct graphs for the lemonade-stand profit using Lynn's and Teiko's equations. What do you notice about the graphs?

Share

Were the two profit equations the same? Write an explanation to justify your response, being sure to refer to the graphical representations that you have constructed.

Lynn says, "This shows that $15x - 3x$ is always equal to $12x$." Do you agree? Justify your thinking.

Extend

Burt wonders if $15x - 2.5x$ is the same as $12.5x$. Create an argument, using graphical representations with the TI-80, to convince Burt that his statement is correct or incorrect.

APPLYING
ACTIVITY 1-25

Economy Class

The economy cabins of some models of DC-10 jet airliners have two seats on the left of the first aisle, five seats in the middle, and two seats on the right of the second aisle. Also the number of rows of seats in the middle is always one more than the number of rows on each of the two sides as shown. How many seats does the economy cabin have if the number of rows in the middle is 34? 45? r?

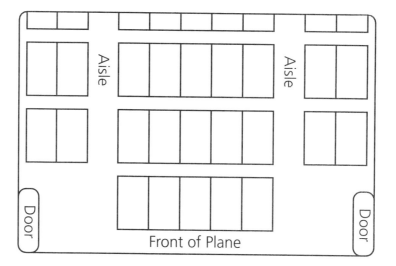

Front of Plane

Investigate

Find the number of economy seats if there are 34 middle rows. What if there are 45 middle rows? In each case, how many rows of side seats are there?

Apply the process you used above to determine the number of rows of side seats when there are r rows of middle seats. Then find the total number of seats in the economy cabin when there are r rows of middle seats.

Share

Explain how to find the number of economy seats when there are r rows of middle seats.

In as many ways as you can, write expressions for the number of economy seats when there are r rows of middle seats. Show that these expressions are equivalent.

Extend

If a DC-10 jet airliner has an economy cabin seating capacity of 239, find the number of rows of seats in the middle and on the sides. Explain how you determined the result.

APPLYING
ACTIVITY 1-26

A Bowling Tournament

> The girls in Eagle Junction Junior High School participate in a bowling tournament in which every girl plays every other girl exactly once. Find a way to determine the number of games to be played when various numbers of girls register for the tournament. If x is the number of girls who register for the tournament and n is the number of games to be played, find a relationship between n and x.

Investigate   Look for a pattern that enables you to find a relationship between n and x.

Share   What is the relationship between n and x? Write an explanation to indicate how you found the relationship.

If you were to construct a graph of the relationship between n and x, what shape would it be? Use your TI-80 to verify your response.

Extend   In a TV interview about the Eagle Junction ten-pin bowling tournament, the director of the tournament stated that 990 games were played. Is this sufficient information to determine precisely how many students played? Explain your reasoning.

APPLYING
ACTIVITY 1-27

Brent's Savings Plan

Brent has a new savings plan. Each week he puts twice as much money into his savings account as he did the week before. If he deposits $1 at the beginning of the first week, determine a way to find how much he will deposit into his savings account at the beginning of various numbers of weeks. If *d* is the number of dollars put into his account at the beginning of week *x*, find a relationship between *d* and *x*.

Investigate   Look for a pattern that enables you to find a relationship between *d* and *x*.

Share   What is the relationship between *d* and *x*? Write an explanation to indicate how you found the relationship.

In Brent's situation, 2 is said to be the *growth factor*. Why is growth factor an appropriate term to use? How is growth factor, as used in Brent's saving plan, different from slope, as used in a relationship such as $y = 2x$?

Extend   After he has made the deposit at the beginning of week *x*, how much money will be in the savings account?

ACTIVITY 1-28 | # Graphing Brent's Savings Plan

> Refer to Brent's Savings Plan, and use the TI-80 to construct a graph that shows the relationship between *d* and *x*, where *d* dollars are deposited into Brent's account at the beginning of week *x*. Is *d* growing at a constant rate?

Investigate

Use Calculator Help 10: Graphing a Function and an appropriate window choice to graph the relationship between *d* and *x*. Use TRACE or some other calculator feature to explore properties of the relationship.

Share

Describe any special characteristics of your graph. For instance, is the graph growing at a constant rate? Does it intersect either axis?

In this graph, the growth factor was 2. Predict how the graph would change if the growth factor were 5. Check your prediction using the TI-80.

Extension

After Brent has saved $500, he stops making deposits and begins to withdraw his money. He takes out $\frac{1}{5}$ of his money at the beginning of the first week, $\frac{1}{5}$ of what is left at the beginning of the second week, $\frac{1}{5}$ of what now remains at the beginning of the third week, and so on. How much will he withdraw at the beginning of week *x*? Explain your thinking and include some discussion about the growth factor in these withdrawals.

Softball Fallout

Peter and Jenny live in a tall apartment complex and are conducting an experiment for their science class. Jenny drops a softball from various floors of the apartment and Peter stands on the ground and uses the stopwatch feature of his digital watch to measure the time it takes for the softball to reach the ground. They construct the following table.

Science Class Data

Time (sec)	1	1.5	2	2.5
Dropping-Point Height (ft)	16	36	64	100

If y represents the drop height in feet and t represents the time in seconds, determine the relationship between y and t. Describe the relationship you found.

Investigate

Look for a pattern that enables you to find a relationship between y and t. Use any of the methods you have considered in this module.

Share

What is the relationship between y and t? Write an explanation to indicate how you found the relationship.

If you were to construct a graph of the relationship between y and t, what shape would it be? Use your TI-80 to verify your response.

Extend

Jenny claims that the speed of the softball in feet per second can be estimated from the data. Is Jenny's claim correct? Write a letter to a friend supporting or disagreeing with Jenny's claim.

CHALLENGING
ACTIVITY 1-30

Fruit Juice and Cookies

In order to raise money for a school concert, Belinda suggested the following idea: On the first day, Belinda will invite two friends for fruit juice and cookies. Each friend will pay 25¢. On the second day, each of Belinda's two friends will invite two more friends for fruit juice and cookies at the same cost. On the third day, each of the four new friends from the second day will invite two more friends, and so on.

If f is the number of friends invited for fruit juice and cookies on the nth day, find a relationship between f and n.

Investigate

Look for a pattern that enables you to find a relationship between f and n. Use any of the methods you have considered in this module.

Share

What is the relationship between f and n? Write an explanation to indicate how you found the relationship.

If you were to construct a graph of the relationship between f and n, what shape would it be? Use your TI-80 to verify your response.

Extend

Determine the total amount of money raised after n days.

Module 2

DATA

Overview

The activities in *Module 2: Data* emphasize organizing, describing, summarizing, and analyzing data. As students explore these activities with a graphics calculator, it is expected that they will achieve greater insights into the patterns, trends, and irregularities of data. In essence, the goal of this module is to develop data sense.

The expected outcomes of Data activities are that students will be able to

- organize data in meaningful ways

- describe and summarize data using various numerical and visual measures

- use technology to construct visual presentations of data

- analyze and interpret data

In order to provide an appropriate development of data analysis for middle-school students, this module has the flexibility to be used as a replacement unit or as a supplemental unit. When used as a replacement unit, we suggest you help students explore consecutively as many of the Developing activities (2-1 to 2-17) as time permits within a given grade level. You may find it helpful to present your own problems and data sets that either relate to the Developing activities or focus on areas in which your students need additional experiences. This approach allows you to use some of the Applying and the Challenging activities as projects, or, alternatively, to use the Applying and the Challenging activities in subsequent years.

If *Module 2: Data* serves as a supplemental unit, you could have students explore data analysis using the Applying activities of the module (2-18 to 2-26). Alternatively, students could first explore Developing activities that incorporate key mathematical concepts that have not been adequately developed in the students' textbook. If this approach is used, the Challenging activities (2-27 to 2-28) would make ideal projects or assessment tasks.

Use the content background (pages 51–56) for your own review of statistics concepts and vocabulary. Information on presenting the student activities (pages 66–93) begins on page 57.

Outline of Key Mathematical Ideas

DEVELOPING ACTIVITIES

	KEY MATHEMATICAL IDEAS
2-1 How Long Are Your Sneakers?	ordering data
2-2 Spreading the Sneaker Message	patterns in the data
2-3 Breaking Down the Sneaker Data	organizing data into categories
2-4 Picturing Sneaker Length	histograms
2-5 Picturing Sneaker Size	comparing histograms
2-6 Boxing the Sneaker Length Data	box plots
2-7 Boxing the Sneaker Size Data	interpreting box plots
2-8 Music Money Makers	mean and median
2-9 Does the Average Change?	effect of extreme values
2-10 Boxing the Top-Grossing 1995 US Tours	interpreting box plots
2-11 Top-Grossing US Tours in 1995 and 1994	comparing box plots
2-12 Scoring an Ice-Skating Competition	using the mean
2-13 Box Plots and Ice-Skating Competition	comparing box plots
2-14 Ice-Skating Competition and the Standard Deviation	standard deviation
2-15 Delving into Middle School Basketball Data	trends in 2-variable data
2-16 Finding Relationships: Basketball Data	scatter plots
2-17 More Relationships in Basketball Data	interpreting scatter plots

APPLYING ACTIVITIES

	KEY MATHEMATICAL IDEAS
2-18 Movie Running Times	entering data
2-19 Ordering the Movie Running Times	ordering data
2-20 Running-Times Data Patterns	patterns in data
2-21 Picturing the Movie Running Times	histograms
2-22 Another Picture of Movie Running Times	box plots
2-23 Do Weeks Shown Depend on Movie Running Times?	scatter plots
2-24 Population Density of 10 US Cities	analyzing 2-variable data
2-25 Population Density and Percentage Unemployed	analyzing 2-variable data
2-26 Sighting a Line of Best Fit	fitting lines

CHALLENGING ACTIVITIES

	KEY MATHEMATICAL IDEAS
2-27 Sneakers Revisited	making predictions: 2-variable data
2-28 Two-Phone-Line Homes on the Rise	making predictions: 2-variable data

Content Background

One-Variable Data Looking at data in their raw form, it is often difficult to detect patterns and trends. An unorganized data set does not lend itself to appropriate description and summary.

For example, a World Wide Web location called HitsWorld posts ratings of popular music. The data in Figure 1 (below) show ratings and other information for the top 20 pop titles for the week ending May 18, 1996. Column L2 shows the total number of weeks each pop title has been on the HitsWorld Top 20 rating. How can you organize these data so that they would be easier to analyze and interpret?

An initial way is to order the data set, that is, to arrange the data in either ascending order or descending order. Figure 2 shows the data from L2 rewritten in descending order.

FIGURE 1

HitsWorld Popular Music: Week Ending May 18, 1996

Title	Artist	L1	L2	L3	L4
Because You Loved Me	Celine Dion	1	9	9	3
Ironic	Alanis Morissette	2	10	2	1
Always Be My Baby	Mariah Carey	3	9	3	4
Nobody Knows	Tony Rich Project	4	13	1	11
Give Me One Good Reason	Tracey Chapman	5	4	5	10
Follow You Down	Gin Blossoms	6	6	5	10
Killing Me Softly	Fugees	7	3	7	15
Closer to Free	Bodeans	8	9	6	27
Wonder	Natilie Merchant	9	13	5	24
Missing	Everything But the Girl	10	22	2	29
Old Man and Me	Hootie and the Blowfish	11	2	11	23
Don't Cry	Seal	12	12	8	33
The World I Know	Collective Soul	13	14	12	31
Insensitive	Jann Arden	14	4	14	35
Be My Lover	La Bouche	15	15	5	42
1, 2, 3, 4 (Sumpin' New)	Coolio	16	3	16	34
Time	Hootie and the Blowfish	17	17	2	45
Sittin' Up in My Room	Brandy	18	8	10	46
Count on Me	W. Houston, CeCe Winans	19	2	16	40
Chains	Tina Arena	20	1	20	48

L1: TW Pop 20—This Week's Rating on HitsWorld Pop 20

L2: NW Pop 20—Number of Weeks Rated on HitsWorld Pop 20

L3: BR Pop 20—Best Rating on HitsWorld Pop 20

L4: TW Top 50—This Week's Rating on HitsWorld Internet Top 50

FIGURE 2

HitsWorld Popular Music: Week Ending May 18, 1996

Title	Artist	Weeks on Hits World Pop 20
Missing	Everything But the Girl	22
Time	Hootie and the Blowfish	17
Be My Lover	La Bouche	15
The World I Know	Collective Soul	14
Nobody Knows	Tony Rich Project	13
Wonder	Natilie Merchant	13
Don't Cry	Seal	12
Ironic	Alanis Morissette	10
Because You Loved Me	Celine Dion	9
Always Be My Baby	Mariah Carey	9
Closer to Free	Bodeans	9
Sittin' Up in My Room	Brandy	8
Follow You Down	Gin Blossoms	6
Give Me One Good Reason	Tracey Chapman	4
Insensitive	Jann Arden	4
Killing Me Softly	Fugees	3
1, 2, 3, 4 (Sumpin' New)	Coolio	3
Old Man and Me	Hootie and the Blowfish	2
Count on Me	W. Houston and CeCe Winans	2
Chains	Tina Arena	1

When this ordering is done, it enables us to easily see that the range of data values is from 22 weeks to 1 week, and that the only real gap in the data is between the top two titles, from 22 to 17 weeks. This also suggests that 22 weeks is an extreme value, or outlier, of the data. Finally, this ordered data set is helpful in constructing various visual displays as well as in determining statistics associated with the location, spread, and shape of the data set.

Centers of the Distribution A data set or distribution of values may have more than one center. On some occasions, the median, or middle number, is used as the center. On other occasions, the mean, or arithmetic average, is used. Sometimes the mode, or most frequent value, is used. In some data sets, two or more of these measures are the same. Any or all of these centers of the distribution can be used to describe the data set.

Figure 3 shows how to determine these three centers of a distribution.

FIGURE 3

Centers of a Distribution: Weeks on HitsWorld

Median: middle value, given as MED in TI-80 menus

1, 2, 2, 3, 3, 4, 4, 6, 8, 9, 9, 9, 10, 12, 13, 13, 14, 15, 17, 22

$$\text{median} = \frac{9+9}{2} = 9 \text{ weeks}$$

Mean: arithmetic average, given by $\bar{x}$ in TI-80 menus

$$\text{mean} = \frac{1+2+2+3+3+4+4+6+8+9+9+9+10+12+13+13+14+15+17+}{22}$$

$$= \frac{176}{20}$$

$$= 8.8 \text{ weeks}$$

Mode: most frequently occuring value

mode = 9 weeks

Notes

1. Because the data set has an even number of values, the median is the mean of the two middle data values, that is, the mean of the 10th and 11th data values in this set.

2. If the first value, 22 weeks, were omitted, there would be an odd number of values. The median would then be the middle value in the data set. Here, it is 9 weeks

3. For some data sets, there may be more than one mode. In these cases, the data are multimodal. Conversely, some data sets may have no mode.

4. Only the mean is affected by the extreme values. To see the impact, replace 22 weeks with 40 weeks and recalculate the mean, median, and mode. The median and the mode both remain 9 weeks, but the mean becomes 9.7 weeks.

FIGURE 4

Measures of Spread: Weeks on HitsWorld

Range: the difference between the maximum and minimum data values

$$= 22 \text{ (maximum)} - 1 \text{ (minimum)}$$
$$= 21 \text{ weeks}$$

Interquartile Range (IQR): the difference between the 75th percentile (upper quartile) and the 25th percentile (lower quartile)

Step 1 Find the median, the 50th percentile, of the data set, and then find the median of each half of the data set. The median of the lower half is the lower quartile (the 25th percentile) and the median of the upper half is the upper quartile (the 75th percentile).

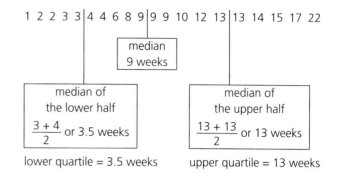

lower quartile = 3.5 weeks   upper quartile = 13 weeks

Step 2 Subtract the lower quartile from the upper quartile.

13 − 3.5
interquartile range = 9.5 weeks

Standard Deviation: the square root of the mean of the sum of the squared deviations about the mean

Step 1 Determine the mean of the data set. It is 8.8.

Step 2 Determine the deviation from the mean for each data value. For example, $(1 - 8.8 = {}^{-}7.8$ is the deviation from the mean for the first value.

Step 3 Square each deviation. For example, $({}^{-}7.8)^2 = 60.84$.

Step 4 Sum the squared deviations, calculate the mean of this sum, and take the square root of this mean. Here are the calculations.

$$= \sqrt{\frac{\sum (x - \bar{x})^2}{n}}$$

$$= \sqrt{\frac{(1 - 8.8)^2 + (2 - 8.8)^2 + \cdots + (22 - 8.8)^2}{20}}$$

$$= \sqrt{\frac{629.2}{20}}$$

$$= 5.61$$

Notes

1. When determining the lower quartile as the median of the lower half of the data and the upper quartile as the median of the upper half of the data and there is an odd number of data values, first omit the median of the entire data set.

2. If the data set represents a complete population, as is the case here, then the divisor in the standard deviation formula is n. Alternatively, if the data set is merely a sample from a population, division in the standard deviation formula by $n - 1$ produces a larger, and better, estimate of spread for a sample.

Spread The spread of a data set is a measure of its variability, or the dispersion of the data values about some focal point of the data set. The range describes the spread based on the maximum and minimum values of the data set. The interquartile range measures the spread based on values positioned 25 percent above (the upper quartile) and 25 percent below (the lower quartile) the median of the data set. The standard deviation measures the spread of the data in relation to the mean. Figure 4 demonstrates the calculation of these measures.

Shape The normal, or mound-shaped, distribution serves as the basis for describing the shape of a data set. A normal distribution is a perfectly symmetrical distribution with the median, mode, and mean represented by the same value.

Shapes that deviate from a symmetric distribution often have outliers. Outliers affect the mean of the data, but not the median or the mode. Figure 5 illustrates symmetric and non-symmetric distributions.

FIGURE 5

Distributions of Data Values

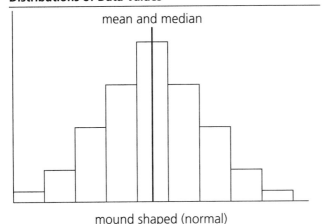

mound shaped (normal)

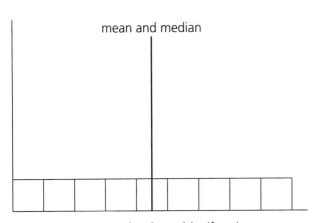

rectangular shaped (uniform)

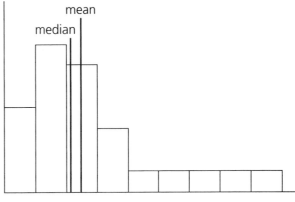

positively skewed (right tail)

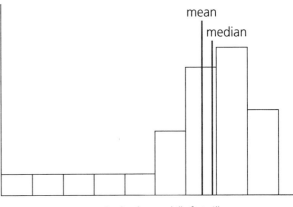

negatively skewed (left tail)

Notes

1. A normal distribution shows perfect symmetry. The mean, the median, and the mode have the same value. Children's sneaker sizes generate a normal distribution.

2. Skewed distributions tail to the right (positive) or tail to the left (negative). Extreme values at either end of the distribution will affect the mean but not the median. Sneaker sizes among sample populations that contain only professional basketball players would produce a negatively skewed distribution.

3. In a uniform distribution, data values are evenly spread across the possible values. The outcomes of one roll of a die, repeated a thousand times, would tend to produce a uniform distribution.

Visual Displays of Data In Module 2: Data, students construct and interpret histograms and box-and-whisker plots. Each of these visual displays has special features that make it valuable for presenting different data sets.

A histogram's key feature is its display of the frequency, or count, of each value or category, or class, of data values. Figure 6 shows several histograms for the Weeks on HitsWorld data from Figure 2.

FIGURE 6

Histograms: Weeks on HitsWorld Data

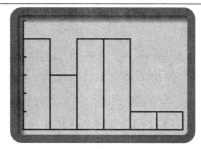

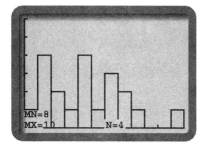

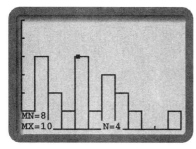

Notes

1. Each of the three TI-80 screens shown above represents the Weeks on HitsWorld data. The first screen shows a class width of 4 weeks, while the other screens both show a class width of 2 weeks.

2. Histograms with narrower class widths tend to reveal more fine-grained features of a data set than do histograms with wider class widths. Histograms with narrower class widths may also tend to over-accentuate characteristics such as clusters, gaps, and outliers.

3. A rule of thumb suggests that division into five or six classes is optimum for data sets with 20 to 30 values. Hence, most statisticians would prefer the first histogram for the Weeks on HitsWorld data.

4. The third screen highlights the TI-80 TRACE feature. On this screen, a flashing cursor highlights the class whose values are 8 or greater but less than 10. The indicator $n = 4$ states that the frequency, or number of values in the class, is 4.

A box-and-whisker plot is constructed using a 5-number summary that anchors markers among the data values. The 5-number summary includes the maximum and minimum data values (the upper extreme and the lower extreme), the upper quartile and the lower quartile, and the median (the 50th percentile). Figure 7 presents a box-and-whisker plot for the data from Weeks on HitsWorld, Figure 2.

FIGURE 7

5-Number Summary: Weeks on HitsWorld Data

Minimum	1 week
Lower Quartile	3.5 weeks
Median	9 weeks
Upper Quartile	13 weeks
Maximum	22 weeks

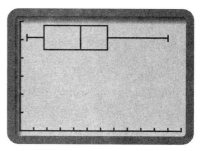

Notes

1. The following steps describe how to construct the box plot from the 5-number summary above.

Step 1 Generate an appropriate number scale (here, 0 to 24 weeks) with equal intervals.

Step 2 Determine the 5-number summary for the data set (see Figure 4).

Step 3 Use the 5-number summary to construct the box and whiskers. Here, the edges of the box go from 3.5 to 13 weeks, namely, the lower and upper quartile values. The whiskers here stretch from 1 to 3.5 weeks (minimum value to the lower quartile) and from 13 to 22 weeks (upper quartile to the maximum value).

Step 4 Draw a line in the box to represent the median value.

2. Screen a on the next page highlights the TI-80 TRACE feature on a box plot. On this screen, a flashing cursor initially highlights the median position. The median value is shown at the bottom of the screen. Using the right and left arrow keys moves the cursor among the values of the 5-number summary.

3. A data set is said to contain an outlier if there are values greater than 1.5 times the interquartile range (see Figure 4) beyond either the lower or upper quartiles. Check that the Weeks on HitsWorld data contain no outliers. Outliers, when they exist, are typically represented with an asterisk on the plot. While the TI-80 does not represent outliers in this way, the TI-83 graphics calculator does make this distinction. Screen **b** below shows the Weeks on HitsWorld data with the maximum value 22 replaced by 30 weeks and a different **XSCL**.

a.

b.

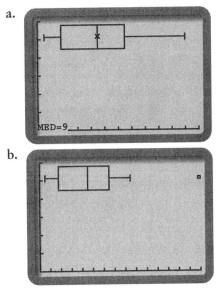

Two-Variable Data The key characteristics of a two-variable, or bivariate, data set are direction, strength, and shape. We can use these characteristics to help describe a data set. Activities in the Data module help students construct scatter plots for bivariate data sets. A scatter plot is a visual display of the data that may reveal characteristics of direction, strength, and shape not apparent from the raw data still in its original form.

Direction Scatter plot a in Figure 8 (next column) provides a visual display of the relationship between data sets L1 and L4 from Figure 1. Data in This Week's Rating on HitsWorld Pop 20 represent x-values, and This Week's Rating on HitsWorld Internet Top 50 represent y-values. If we study the scatter plot, we see that as the Pop 20 rating increases, so does the Top 50 rating. The direction of this relationship is said to be positive because an increase in the values of one variable is associated with an increase in the values of the other variable. A relationship is said to be negative if an increase in the values of one variable is associated with a decrease in the values of the other variable.

FIGURE 8

Scatter Plots: Weeks on HitsWorld Data

a.

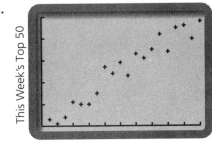

This Week's Pop 20

b.

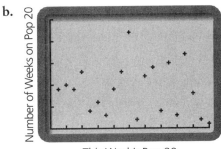

This Week's Pop 20

If we study the relationship between data sets L1 and L2 from Figure 1, This Week's Rating on HitsWorld Pop 20 representing x-values and Number of Weeks Rated on HitsWorld Pop 20 representing y-values, it appears that the relationship is neither positive nor negative. In this case, there is no apparent direction to the relationship. This is illustrated in scatter plot b in Figure 8.

Strength One way to assess the strength of a relationship in a two-variable data set is with the ellipse test, in which an ellipse is drawn as accurately as possible to fully capture the data points. In Figure 9, the ellipse test is applied to the two scatter plots from Figure 8, as well as a third scatter plot, c, which shows the relationship between data sets L1 and L3 from Figure 1, This Week's Rating on HitsWorld Pop 20 (x-values) and Best Rating on HitsWorld Pop 20 (y-values), respectively.

FIGURE 9

Ellipse Tests: Weeks on HitsWorld Data

a.
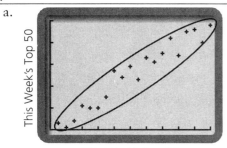

b.
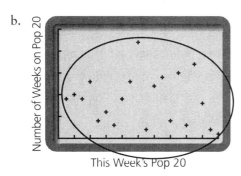

c.
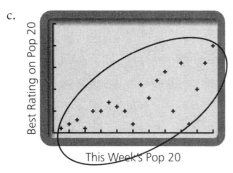

The shape of each ellipse helps us assess the strength of each relationship. In plot a, the ellipse is long and narrow, indicating a moderate to strong linear relationship. In plot b, the ellipse appears nearly circular. Such an ellipse indicates a very weak or non-existent linear relationship between the two variables. The ellipse capturing the points in plot c illustrates a possible linear relationship; however, the relationship is weaker than the one displayed in plot a.

Shape Scatter plots that reveal a linear relationship, such as the one in Figure 9a, represent only one possible shape for a two-variable data set. Figure 10 includes scatter plots of two-variable data sets that are quadratic and exponential. Students can explore quadratic and exponential relationships in the activities of Module 1: Algebra.

FIGURE 10

Scatter Plots: Quadratic and Exponential Relationships

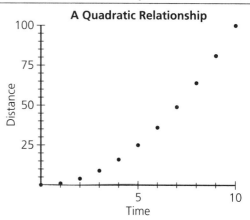

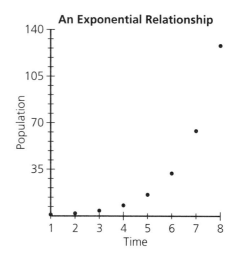

Implementation Notes and Solutions

Developing Activities

ACTIVITY 2-1 (p. 66)   ORDERING DATA

How Long Are Your Sneakers?

Using Data Set 3 (p. 140), this activity and the next focus on ordering data as a way to examine trends and characteristics. You might find it helpful to use probing questions to have students explain why ordering is useful in examining data. Using Calculator Help 2: Sorting Lists, students will find that they can arrange the data in ascending order, `1:sorta(L1)`, or descending order, `2:sortd(L1)`. Such orderings are not only helpful in finding the range of the data, but they are also useful in determining the minimum and maximum values of the data as well as any clusters, gaps, or outliers. Later in the module students can use the sorting functions to determine the median, the mode, and the upper and lower quartiles. Students may need to first consult Calculator Help 1: Entering Lists.

For the Extend, the ordered sneaker-size data can be seen to have a small range (5–13), no gaps or outliers, and largely the same number of students in each of the first five size categories, 7 through 11.

ACTIVITY 2-2 (p. 67)   PATTERNS IN THE DATA

Spreading the Sneaker Message

Students should be encouraged to look for features of the ordered data. For example, it can be observed that the range goes from 24 to 34, there are no outliers, and the data have two gaps because there are no students with sneaker lengths of 25 and 31. These two gaps create three clusters, although some students might reasonably argue that the clusters are more apparent than real and would disappear if another sample or a larger sample were used.

For the Extend, answers will vary. Students might notice that sneaker size data increases as sneaker length data increases, students with a particular sneaker length have the same sneaker size, and the range for sneaker size is slightly less than that for sneaker length. Some students might also wonder whether a student with sneaker length 25 will have a sneaker size of 5, a sneaker size of 6, or some fractional size. This could generate some useful discussion on fractional sneaker sizes.

ACTIVITY 2-3 (p. 68)   ORGANIZING DATA INTO CATEGORIES

Breaking Down the Sneaker Data

Commence this activity by asking students to identify any methods, other than ordering data, of organizing or displaying data. This may well set the stage for Activities 2-3 through 2-7, where histograms and box plots are introduced. Frequencies in the table are: 28–29, 8; 30–31, 3; 32–33, 6; and 34–35, 1. Students might note that the categories with the greatest frequency are toward the middle of the range (26–30) and the categories with the least frequencies are at the ends of the range (24–25, 34–35). Students might also note that the gaps have disappeared under this categorization, because missing sneaker lengths such as 25 and 31 have become part of a larger category. In fact, grouping into categories means that you no longer have all of the information contained in the original data set. For example, you do not know that 25 and 31 are missing.

In the Extend, if students break the sneaker-size data into groups of two, the categories with the greater frequencies will again be toward the middle of the range and those with the lesser frequencies will be toward the ends of the range. The table should give these frequencies: 5–6, 4; 7–8, 7; 9–10, 7; 11–12, 6; and 13–14, 1. Using groups of two, the sneaker-size data have fewer categories and are more uniform in the middle of the range than are the sneaker-length data.

ACTIVITY 2-4 (p. 69)   HISTOGRAMS

Picturing Sneaker Length

The histogram students are to construct is shown on the student page. When using TRACE with the histogram constructed by the TI-80, you will notice that the minimum and maximum values of each category/class are given. Emphasize with students that the minimum value is contained in the class but the maximum is not. The maximum is actually contained in the next class. The table built in Activity 2-3 and the histogram are equivalent representations of the data. If the XSCL, the scale on the *x*-axis, is changed from 2 to 3, the new categories or classes for the table and the histogram will be: 24–27, 27–30, 30–33, and 33–36. This change in XSCL will also change the frequencies and the shape of the histogram. All of the data will be incorporated into this new histogram, but once again it will not be possible to identify each original piece of data.

Picturing Sneaker Size

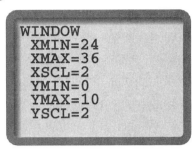

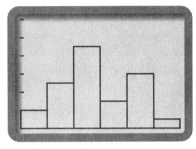

The histogram for sneaker length data shown on Activity 2-4 and repeated here is contrasted with the histogram for sneaker size data (Activity 2-5) shown here.

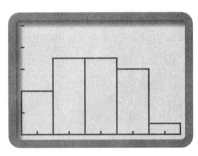

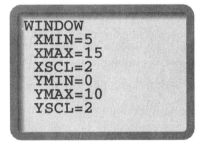

Each histogram displays data for the same set of students. Both histograms use an XSCL of 2, that is they include two different sneaker lengths or sizes. The sneaker-length histogram has more categories or classes than the sneaker-size histogram but is less uniform in the middle of the range. If the XSCL values were different for each histogram, you would tend to lose the correspondence between sneaker length and sneaker size that is contained in the original data. The number of categories, the frequencies, and the shape would be varied in an arbitrary manner. It would be

helpful for students to build a summary of the key characteristics of histograms as well as some of the special considerations that need to be exercised in constructing them with the TI-80.

Boxing the Sneaker-Length Data

The box plot that students are to construct is shown on the student page. The 5-number summary contains the key elements of the box plot and these are the only values that can be read directly from the box plot. For data set A, the 5-number summary is minimum = 1, lower quartile = 2, median = 4, upper quartile = 6, and maximum = 7. For data set B, the 5-number summary is minimum = 1, lower quartile = 2.5, median = 4.5, upper quartile = 6.5, and maximum = 8. In building your own sets of data, you might note that it is more difficult to determine the 5-number summary for sets of data that contain 8, 12, 16, . . . values, because medians and quartiles will be fractions. For background review on the meaning and method of calculating the 5-number summary, refer to Figure 4 in the content background teacher notes, as well as to the discussion on page 52 and page 54.

It would be valuable to have students construct a paper-and-pencil box plot for this data or another set of data so that they fully understand the function of each part of the box plot and also how the number scale relates to the box plot. References to both box and whisker elements and the percentage of the data in each would also be useful at this stage.

Boxing the Sneaker-Size Data

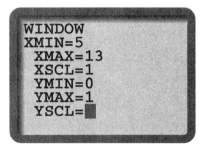

The minimum and maximum are 5 and 13, respectively, while the lower and upper quartiles are 7 and 11, respectively. The median is 9. Since the upper quartile is 11, approximately 75 percent of the students wear a smaller sneaker size than this value. In the Extend, the key point is that the lower quartile is calculated as the median of the data values that are less than the median for the entire data set. This effectively leaves the median for the entire data set out of calculations.

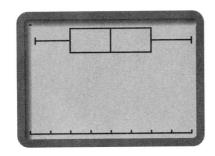

As part of this activity, you might like to have students compare the shapes of the box plots for sneaker size and sneaker length.

ACTIVITY 2-8 (p. 73)   MEAN AND MEDIAN

Music Money Makers

Using Data Set 4 (page 142) this activity and Activity 2-9 consider centers of a distribution, such as the mean and the median. You might also want to introduce the mode as the value which occurs most frequently in a data set. The values for the mean and median calculated by the TI-80 Graphics Calculator are shown in the activity. The median is the middle value when the data values are written in ascending or descending order. In this case, because there are 10 data values the median is the mean of the fifth and sixth data values, that is,

$\frac{34.0 + 34.1}{2} = 34.05$. The Extend is very helpful in

having students realize that if a new data set is formed by changing every data value in the original data set to the mean, then the sum of the values in both the original and the new data sets are the same. This result builds a better understanding of the mean and also justifies the use of the formula:

$$\text{mean} = \frac{\text{sum of the data values}}{\text{number of data values}}$$

ACTIVITY 2-9 (p. 74)   EFFECTS OF EXTREME VALUES

Does the Average Change?

It is hoped that students will be able to predict that the change in The Eagles' gross earnings will affect the mean but not the median. Because The Eagles' data value is the greatest data value, it will affect neither the order of the data values nor the identity of the middle values. On the other hand, change will certainly decrease the sum of the data and, hence, the mean. The adjusted mean is 31.36 million. The same is true for the Share, where the mean is 30.13 million. For the Extend, the mean of the 11 data values with Jimmy Buffet included is 32.29 million. This means that the sum of the 11 data values (including Jimmy Buffet) is 32.29 × 11 = 355.19 million. The sum of the 10 data values (excluding Buffet) is 33.92 × 10 = 339.2 million. This means that Jimmy Buffet grossed

355.19 – 339.2 = 16 million. You might also encourage students to make up their own data sets to show the influence of very high or very low data values.

ACTIVITY 2-10 (p. 75)   INTERPRETING BOX PLOTS

Boxing the Top-Grossing 1995 US Tours

You might want to have students explore these activities after Activity 2-7 because they extend students' understanding of box plots. We felt it was valuable to look more carefully at the mean, median, and quartiles before introducing a more precise rule for outliers. The box plot and its window dimensions for the 10 Top-Grossing 1995 US Rock Tours are shown here.

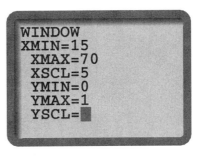

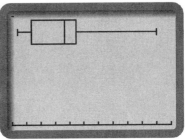

The lower and upper quartiles are 22.8 million and 36.9 million, respectively, and the minimum and maximum are 17.3 million and 65.6 million, respectively. The median is 34.05 million. Both quartiles are contained in the set, because the data sets for which they are medians contain an odd number of values, 5. The median is not in the set, because the data set for which it is calculated contains an even number of values, 10. Thus, the median is the mean of the two middle values.

Because the lower quartile is 22.8 million and the upper quartile is 36.9 million, 50 percent of the data lies between these two values. For the Extend, we find that 1.5 times the length of the box is 1.5 × 14.1 = 21.2. This means that the division point for the upper outliers, sometimes called the upper fence, is 36.9 + 21.2 = 58.1. Because this fence value is less than 65.6 we see that The Eagles' gross earnings is an upper outlier. There are no lower outliers.

Top-Grossing US Tours in 1995 and 1994

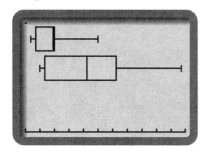

The box plots for the Top-Grossing US Tours in 1995 and 1994 are shown here. It is important for students to note the ranges and scales under WINDOW must be adjusted so that the numbers fit both box plots. The range needs to include 17.3, the minimum for 1995 data, and 124.2, the maximum for 1994 data. They can also use ► and ◄ (without using TRACE) to generate the corresponding number line values on the box plots. Use ▲ and ▼ to move from one box plot to the other.

The minimum and maximum for 1995 are 17.3 million and 65.6 million, while the lower and upper quartiles are 22.8 million and 36.9 million. The 1995 median is 34.05 million, and the mean is 33.92 million. For 1994, the minimum and maximum are 23.3 million and 124.2 million, while the lower and upper quartiles are 27.0 million and 75.8 million. The 1994 median is 57.85 million, and the mean is 61.93 million. The interquartile ranges are 14.1 million and 48.8 million.

Scoring an Ice-Skating Competition

Using Data Set 5 on page 143, this activity and the next two look at the spread of data sets. Before starting this activity, ask students how they would measure the spread of a data set. If possible, use their ideas to launch the activities on spread and dispersion. The Problem in this activity is intended to stimulate student discussion and to generate several solutions. In most sporting contests that involve this kind of scoring—gymnastics, swimming, and water ballet, for instance—the mean of the judges' scores is usually used to determine the winner. In this case, Caterina and Cristie would have tied because their means are both 8. The same result occurs if the median is used, as once again both have a median of 8. Given the fact that both skaters have the same mean and median, it is conceivable that a judge may have decided in favor of Caterina because her range of scores (9 – 7 = 2) is less than that of Cristie (10 – 6 = 4), even though both have the same interquartile range, 2. The Extend describes the process used in major competitions such as the

Olympic Games. Under this method, using truncated means, or means which have been rounded down to a given decimal place, the two skaters would still have tied. It would be a brave judge who would separate these two skaters.

Box Plots and Ice-Skating Competition

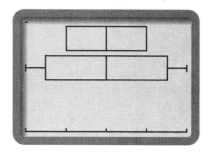

The box plots for Caterina's and Cristie's scores are shown here. Caterina's box plot has no whiskers and this emphasizes more strongly the fact that her range of scores is very small. The 5-number summaries for the women are: Caterina: MAX, 9; MIN, 7; Med, 8; UQ, 9; LQ, 7; and Christie: MAX, 10; MIN, 6; Med, 8; UQ, 9.5; LQ, 6.5. Students should note that the minimum score for Caterina is the same as the lower quartile and her maximum score is the same as the upper quartile, so there are no whiskers. The two box plots have the same median, but their ranges are different. The box plots also have different lower-quartile and upper-quartile values and different IQRs.

Ice-Skating Competition and Standard Deviation

Even though the treatment of standard deviation is not intended to be extensive or deep, you may choose to omit this section. None of the subsequent activities depend on this one. Encourage students to think of standard deviation like other measures of spread, even though it is more complex to calculate. Keep the calculations to a minimum by using the features of the TI-80. The standard deviations, calculated using the TI-80, are shown in the activity. Because this should be regarded as a sample of scores, Caterina's standard deviation is 1 and Cristie's standard deviation is 1.58. The standard deviations are measures of spread and, in this case, produce interpretations similar to those based on the range and interquartile range. Cristie's scores are more spread about the mean than are Caterina's. Answers will vary for the Extend. For example, the set of values 10, 9, 7, 7, 7 has a mean of 8 and a standard deviation of 1.41.

Delving into Middle School Basketball Data

Using Data Set 6 page 144, this is the first of a series of activities that deal with *multi-variable data*, a data set that contains more than one piece of data for each person or element. It is important for you to encourage students to look at the trends in the data in various ways, including any relationships between the variables. The Hawks had more fouls (16) than the Bluebirds did (14). The Hawks won the game by a score of 41 to 36.

For the Extend, it is possible to determine how long the game lasted. Students could conjecture that the game time was 20 minutes and show that this works for both teams. A second way is to note that the total time on the bench for Bluebird players is 40 minutes. Because 40 minutes represents the amount of time two Bluebird players are off the court, the time period must be $40 \div 2 = 20$ minutes. A third, more rigorous solution, using the Bluebird data, is to say that the first five Bluebird players sat out for a total of 18 minutes and this playing time was provided by Amanda and Putu. Hence $(x - 10) + (x - 12) = 18$, where x is the total playing time. This results in $x = 20$. A fourth solution, similar to the third, uses the total time played by the seven Bluebird players and equates that to the total time 5 players are on the floor. This leads to the equation: $(x - 2) + (x - 4) + (x - 4) + (x - 6) + (x - 2) + (x - 10) + (x - 12) = 5x$, again producing a solution of 20 minutes.

Finding Relationships in Basketball Data

A scatter plot is one of the most effective ways to observe relationships between two variables. You might find some of the following probes helpful in asking students to describe their scatter plots:

- Do the points lie on a straight line?

- Do the points lie on a curve?

- Suppose you drew an ellipse, or oval, to enclose all the points of the scatter plot. Would you describe the ellipse as long and narrow or nearly circular?

In this activity, the scatter plot for total points scored versus time spent on the bench is presented on the student page. This would be a useful time to discuss *dependent variable*, that which depends upon the value of other variable, and *independent variable*, that which determines the value of the other. Here, we assume that total points scored depend on time spent on the bench, so the total number of points scored represents the dependent variable and time on the bench represents

the independent variable. In fact, in this problem, as the time on the bench increases, the total number of points scored decreases. Notice how this is shown by the fall of the points from left to right. Students might claim that the points in the scatter plot lie approximately on a straight line, so the relationship is linear. Alternatively, others might justifiably claim that the points lie along a curve, so the relationship is non-linear.

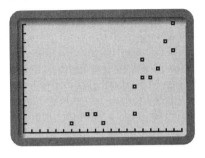

Scatter plot of playing time, x, vs total points scored, y, for the middle school basketball data.

For the Extend, the scatter plot is shown here. The shape of the two scatter plots is similar, but in this one, the total number of points scored increase as the playing times increase. Some students might also notice that the two scatter plots are mirror images, or reflections, of each other.

More Relationships in Basketball Data

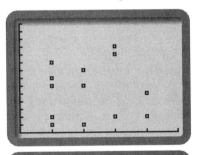

Scatter plot of number of fouls, x, versus total points scored, y

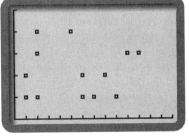

Scatter plot of total points scored, x, versus number of fouls, y

In this activity, we have assumed that the total number of points scored depends on the number of fouls because fouls tend to limit scoring. However, it would also be possible to justify using number of fouls as the dependent variable and total points scored as the independent variable in the sense that fouls were produced by aggressive scoring. The two possible scatter plots are shown here. Some students may notice that one scatter plot reflected over the line $y = x$ gives the other. The scatter plots indicate that there is very little relationship between the two variables. Notice how the shape of the points on the scatter plot is nearly circular, and that a given number of fouls can be associated with different total numbers of points scored, including both low and high values.

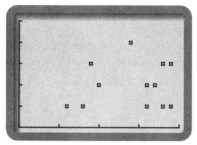

Scatter plot of playing time in minutes, x, versus number of fouls, y, for middle-school basketball

The scatter plot for the Extend is also shown here. There appears to be a relationship between number of fouls and playing time in minutes, but it is a non-linear relationship. The scatter plot suggests that basketball players who have very short or very long playing times have fewer fouls. Players with longer time on the floor may be instructed by their coaches to be less aggressive in order to keep out of foul trouble. Our solution shows number of fouls as the dependent variable. Students could also justify that playing time is the dependent variable.

Applying Activities

Activities 2-18 through 2-23 review the key ideas introduced in the Developing Activities. However, these applications are designed so that students take more initiative in developing their own solutions. There is strong emphasis on having students share their thinking with each other, as well as on writing about their solutions. Some of the applications may be used as assessment tasks.

Activities 2-24 through 2-26 provide a valuable experience in using multi-variable data because students must develop a new variable (population density) from existing variables. Teachers might like to develop additional data sets incorporating this feature. For example, a data set involving distance and time can generate speed, one involving cost and weight can generate unit cost, one involving points scored and time played in basketball can generate points per minute or scoring potency. You may also use these activities as a project for assessment.

ACTIVITY 2-18 (p. 83)　　　　　　　ENTERING DATA

Movie Running Times

There are several ways to enter the Movie Running Times data (page 145) into the TI-80. The responses

1.30 hours and 130 minutes are inappropriate because neither is equivalent to 1 hour 30 minutes. Students will notice that when data are entered into L2 as a mixed number, the calculator automatically represents this as a decimal.

ACTIVITY 2-19 (p. 84)　　　　　　　ORDERING DATA

Ordering the Movie Running Times

Students can order the Movie Running Times data in ascending or descending order using the calculator's sort features. For the Extend, it is useful to enter the data in minutes and then sort the data. Mathematical operations will have the same effect on the data as long as numerically equivalent representations of the data are used.

ACTIVITY 2-20 (p. 85)　　　　　　PATTERNS IN THE DATA

Running-Times Data Patterns

The minimum value for the data set is 78 minutes for Balto, and the maximum value is 172 minutes for Heat, so the range is 94 minutes. Students could enter the data in hours but this is more cumbersome. Both Heat and Casino appear to be outliers and this can be confirmed by using the $1.5 \times$ IQR criterion described in Figure 7. For the Extend, several answers are possible. Here is one solution.

Day 1: 172 minutes for *Heat* and
　　　　170 minutes for *Casino*

Day 2: 97 minutes for *Four Rooms*,
　　　　133 minutes for *Assassins*,
　　　　129 minutes for *GoldenEye*

Day 3: 124 minutes for *Sabrina*,
　　　　123 minutes for *Waiting to Exhale*,
　　　　101 minutes for *Grumpier Old Men*

Day 4: 123 minutes for *Cutthroat Island*,
　　　　115 minutes for *American President*,
　　　　110 minutes for *Sudden Death*

Day 5: 102 minutes for *Now and Then*,
　　　　104 minutes for *Jumanji*,
　　　　106 minutes for *Father of the Bride II*

Day 6: 93 minutes for *Gold Diggers*,
　　　　78 minutes for *Balto*,
　　　　81 minutes for *Toy Story*

Day 7: 93 minutes for *Tom and Huck*,
　　　　91 minutes for *Ace Ventura*,
　　　　90 minutes for *Dracula*

The least number of days required is 7, because the mean number of hours needed to watch the movies in 6 days is 6.2 hours.

Picturing the Movie Running Times

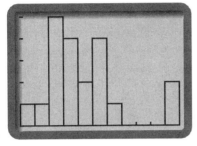

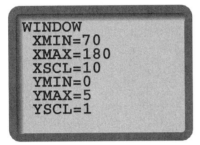

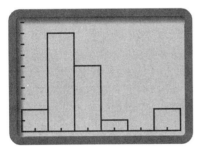

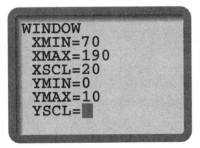

The histogram with class width 10 minutes confirms that Heat and Casino are outliers and that there is a gap in the data between 133 and 170 minutes. The histogram also reveals that approximately 75 percent of the running times lie between 90 minutes and 130 minutes. The histogram with class width 20 reveals similar information about outliers and gaps to the

histogram with class width 10. However, in moving from the histogram with class width 10 to the one with class width 20, the sharper discriminations between classes, such as the small number of movie running times between 110 and 120 minutes, are lost. For the Extend, 35 percent of the movie running times are greater than 2 hours. Students could count or use one of the histograms to solve the Extend.

Another Picture of Movie Running Times

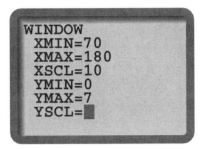

The screen with both the histogram and box plot for the Movie Running Times data is shown here, together with the window dimensions used to create the plots. In response to the first question in Share, 50 percent of the movies run longer than 105 minutes. This is most easily determined from the median of the box plot, identified by using TRACE. A useful approximation can be obtained from the histogram, for more than 50 percent of the movies run longer than 100 minutes. For the second question in Share, the histogram must be used. Again using TRACE, we see that 18 of 20 movies (90%) are 90 minutes or longer. Students should note that the shape of the histogram provides useful information about the distribution of classes of running times and also allows percentages of running times above and below a given value to be approximated. 50 percent of the movies run longer than 104 minutes, and 90 percent of the movies run longer than 129 minutes.

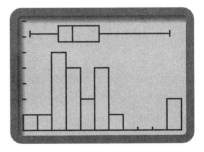

The box plot does not provide useful information on individual running times or classes of running times, but is helpful in identifying key values, such as the median, quartiles, and extreme values. The box plot is also useful in talking about certain ranges of data values, such as the lower or upper 25 percent and the middle 50 percent. Because 1 hour 50 minutes, or 110 minutes, is not one of the 5-number-summary values, the histogram will give a better approximation in the Extend. Using the histogram with class width 10, the percentage is approximately 45.

ACTIVITY 2-23 (p. 88) SCATTER PLOTS

Do Weeks Shown Depend on Movie Running Times?

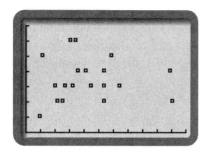

Here is a scatter plot showing the relationship between number of weeks shown (dependent variable) and running time (independent variable). The scatter plot indicates that there is a moderate linear relationship between the two variables, with number of weeks shown increasing as the running time increases. About four or five points from the scatter plot could be located on a line of best fit, or a line which best approximates the trend in the data. In the Extend, answers will vary depending on where students place their line of best fit. A good approximation would be about 3.5 weeks.

ACTIVITY 2-24 (p. 89) ANALYZING 2-VARIABLE DATA

Population Density of 10 US Cities

Activity 2-24 uses the measure of population density to investigate 2-variable data (Data Set 8 page 146). The population densities run from 2475 people per square mile for Corpus Christi to 12,209 people per square mile for Chicago. Fifty percent (50%) of the cities have population densities less than 4,000 people per square mile, and 80 percent have population densities less than 8,000 people per square mile. Only Miami and Chicago have population densities greater than 10,000 people per square mile. In the Extend, Boris's method is not especially useful because it is not meaningful to subtract two unlike quantities. The notions of people per square mile and square miles per person do convey a useful measure because they are rates that have visual as well as mathematical meaning.

ACTIVITY 2-25 (p. 90) ANALYZING 1-VARIABLE DATA

Population Density and Percentage Unemployed

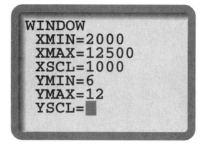

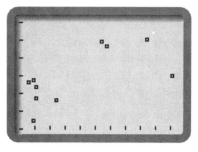

Scatter plot for population density, *x*, vs. percent unemployed, *y*, for 10 US cities.

The scatter plot for population density (independent variable) and percentage unemployed (dependent variable) is shown here, together with the window dimensions used to create the plot. The points show a reasonably good linear relationship in that a line could be drawn close to most points. Students might be encouraged to locate a line of best fit by eye-balling a number of line locations. The best-fit line actually passes through the point $(\bar{x}, \bar{y})$ where $\bar{x}$ is the mean of the x-values and $\bar{y}$ is the mean of the y-values.

Students can either work from the scatter plot or use an appropriate line to show that the unemployment prediction for New York, with population density of 24,327 people per square mile, is about 14.3 percent. Students should discuss the meaningfulness of this prediction, given that the population density for New York City is so much greater than the population density of any city in the original data.

ACTIVITY 2-26 (p. 91) FITTING LINES

Sighting a Line of Best Fit

The procedure for constructing the line is described in the activity and in Calculator Help 8: Line Drawing. Students should use the scatter plot constructed in Activity 2-25. They might also be encouraged to fit their lines through the point $(\bar{x}, \bar{y})$, as explained in the notes for Activity 2-25. In the Extend, some students might be able to find an approximation for the equation of their line and determine the predicted value using this equation. One suitable equation is $y = 0.0007x + 7.3$, yielding an unemployment prediction of about 14.3 percent for New York.

Challenging Activities

Activities 2-27 and 2-28 could both be used as projects for assessment. They involve analysis, writing, and opportunities for students to apply and connect mathematical ideas.

ACTIVITY 2-27 (p. 92)   PREDICTING: 2-VARIABLE DATA

Sneakers Revisited

In this activity, students could construct a scatter plot using sneaker length as the independent variable and sneaker size as the dependent variable. The scatter plot indicates that the two variables have a strong linear relationship. Consequently it is easy to draw a line that is very close to most points. Using the scatter plot or an appropriate line, the prediction for Mark's sneaker size will be about 10.5. The Extend is intended to draw attention to the fact that a sneaker length of 36 centimeters is outside the range of the original data set. Hence students should be more cautious about extrapolating, or inferring additional information that is beyond the range of the data set.

ACTIVITY 2-28 (p. 93)   PREDICTING: 2-VARIABLE DATA

Two-Phone-Line Homes on the Rise

The investigators in this illustration noted that the percentage of homes with multiple phone lines increased by 8.5 percent (16.5 – 8) from 1994 to 1995. They then seem to have assumed that this rate would continue until the year 2000, producing a result of about 59 percent for the year 2000. Students could use a graph or the concept of rate to find this value. During small-group and class discussions, students might discuss how appropriate it is to use just the 1994–1995 change. This one-year growth may be just an aberration. For example, a line fitted through the values for 1990 and 1995 has a smaller slope (2.16) and predicts 27.3 percent for the year 2000 rather than 59 percent. A number of factors might influence the continuing growth of homes with multiple phone lines, including cost of equipment and installation, growth of new technologies requiring multiple phone lines, and percentage of people who have already installed multiple phone lines. For the Extend, the prediction will be about 11.5 percent, as it is based on a line with the very small slope of 0.58.

DEVELOPING
ACTIVITY 2-1

How Long Are Your Sneakers?

Data Set 3: Sneaker Lengths and Sneaker Sizes, contains information on sneaker lengths and sneaker sizes for a sample of middle-school students. The data are ordered alphabetically. How can you use your calculator to order the data set by sneaker length? What happens to the data set when it is ordered by sneaker length?

Investigate

Enter the sneaker-length data into list L1 of your calculator. You may need to refer to Calculator Help 1: Entering Lists. Then use Calculator Help 2: Sorting Lists to order the data by sneaker length.

Share

Describe what the sort features do to the original data set. How are the sort features alike and how are they different?

Explain why you would want to order a data set such as this one numerically.

Extend

Enter the sneaker size information from Data Set 3 into list L2 and then order the sneaker sizes numerically. What do you observe about this ordered set?

Spreading the Sneaker Message

Describe as you would to a friend the most important characteristics or patterns of the sneaker lengths in Data Set 3.

Investigate

Examine features of the data set. Look for

- the *range*, or difference between the greatest and smallest values
- extraordinary values, or *outliers*
- gaps and clusters

Before you begin your examination, decide whether you should use the alphabetically ordered data set or the numerically ordered data set.

Share

Write a letter to your friend to describe the most important characteristics or patterns in the sneaker lengths. Share your letter with your classmates.

Extend

Use the sneaker lengths and sneaker sizes information in Data Set 3. Compare the data on sneaker sizes with the corresponding data on sneaker lengths. What similarities do you notice? What differences are there?

Breaking Down the Sneaker Data

Your friend suggested another way to describe the characteristics or patterns in the sneaker-length data. She constructed a table to show the number, or *frequency*, of students who have sneaker lengths in various categories, such as 24–25, 26–27, . . ., 34–35. How does the table bring out some of the patterns in the data? What information about the original data set is not contained in the table?

Sneaker Lengths

Lengths	Frequency
24–25	2
26–27	5
28–29	
30–31	
32–33	
34–35	

Investigate

Your friend started the table shown here. Complete the table.

Share

What patterns does the table bring out in the data? Were these patterns apparent in the original data set or in the numerically ordered data set? Explain.

What information about the original data set is not contained in the table?

Extend

Construct a table for the sneaker-size data that organizes it by categories, or *classes*. Include two consecutive sizes in each category. Your first category is 5–6.

Now compare the category tables for the sneaker-length data and the sneaker-size data. How are they alike? How are they different?

DEVELOPING
ACTIVITY 2-4

Picturing Sneaker Length

The calculator provides yet another way to display the sneaker-length data in classes. It does this by constructing a *histogram*, a graph which displays frequencies of an event. How can you use your calculator to construct a histogram of the sneaker-length data? How does the histogram relate to the table you created?

Investigate

Be sure the sneaker-length data are in list L1 of your calculator. Use Calculator Help 3: Histogram to create the histogram using these directions.

- Set the window using the values shown here.
- Define and display the histogram according to the steps described in the calculator help.

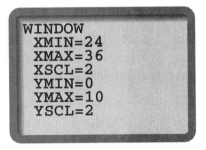 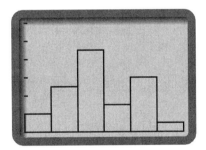

Your histogram should look like the one shown here.

Share

In setting the range on your calculator, you keyed in *x*-values and *y*-values. What do the *x*-values stand for? What do the *y*-values stand for? Why were the window values shown above chosen for this data set?

Examine the histogram and carefully describe what it says about the sneaker-length data. In examining the histogram, you may find it helpful to use TRACE and ◀ or ▶ on your calculator.

How does the histogram relate to the table you created in Breaking Down the Sneaker Data?

Extend

Suppose the XSCL value in the window is 3 instead of 2. Predict how this will change your histogram. Change the XSCL to 3. View the new histogram and observe any changes.

- Were the changes in line with your prediction?
- Were all of the data shown in the new histogram? Explain.

Picturing Sneaker Size

Use your calculator to create a histogram of the sneaker-size information in Data Set 3. Create categories that include two consecutive sizes in each category. Your first category is 5-6.

How does the sneaker-size histogram relate to the sneaker-length histogram?

Investigate   Be sure the sneaker-size data are in list L2 of your calculator. Construct a histogram for the sneaker-size data using Stat Plot 2 to define the histogram. Take care in choosing values for the window. Use an XSCL of 2 as you did in Activity 3-4.

Share   Describe how you set the window for your histogram.

Compare the sneaker-length histogram (Stat Plot 1) with the sneaker-size histogram (Stat Plot 2). How are they alike? How are they different? Are your answers consistent with your responses to Extend in Picturing Sneaker Length? Explain.

Extend   Suppose you had used different XSCL values for the sneaker-length histogram (Stat Plot 1) and the sneaker-size histogram (Stat Plot 2). How would this affect your comparison of the two histograms? Explain.

DEVELOPING
ACTIVITY 2-6
Boxing the Sneaker-Length Data

Another type of visual display used to represent data is a *box-and-whisker plot*, often called a *box plot*. How can you use the calculator to construct a box plot for the sneaker-length data in Data Set 3? What are the key elements of a box plot?

Investigate

Be sure the sneaker-length data are in list L1 of your calculator. Use Calculator Help 4: Box Plot to create your plot using these directions.

```
WINDOW
  XMIN=24
  XMAX=36
  XSCL=1
  YMIN=0
  YMAX=1
  YSCL=1
```

- Set the window using the values shown here.
- Define and display the box plot according to the steps described in the calculator help.

Your plot should look like the one shown here. The five numbers used to construct a box plot are highlighted on the last screen. Use the ◄ TRACE key and then the left and right arrow keys (◄ , ►) to find these five values. Look for relationships between the five values and the numerically ordered sneaker-length data.

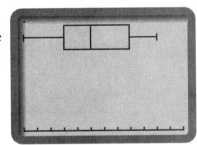
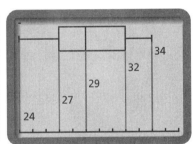

Share

Describe how you found from the ordered data the five numbers used to construct the box plot. Why do you think these numbers are called the *five-number summary*: minimum, lower quartile, median, upper quartile, and maximum? Explain.

How do you think a box plot can be constructed once you have identified the five-number-summary values? Explain how to create the box and explain how to create each whisker. (Hint: Look back at the box plot on your calculator and see if you can identify a number line. How was that used?)

Extend

Data Sets	
Data Set A	1, 2, 3, 4, 5, 6, 7
Data Set B	1, 2, 3, 4, 5, 6, 7, 8

Find the five-number summary for each of the data sets in the table.

Was it more difficult to find the five-number summary for one of the sets? Explain.

Boxing the Sneaker-Size Data

Construct a box plot for the sneaker-size data. Use it to determine the percentage of students who wear a sneaker size greater than 7. Find the sneaker size for which 75 percent of the students wear a smaller size.

Investigate

Be sure the sneaker-size data are in list L2 of your calculator. Construct a box plot for the sneaker-size data using Stat Plot 2 to define the box plot. Take care in choosing minimum and maximum values and scale values for the window.

Use TRACE and ◄ ► to find the five-number summary for the box plot. Check these values using the ordered data set for the sneaker-size values.

Share

Use the box plot to tell what percentage of students use a sneaker size larger than 7. How did the shape of the box plot help you determine the percentage? Explain.

Use the box plot to find the sneaker size for which 75 percent of the students wear a smaller size. Justify your response.

Extend

If you look back at the ordered sneaker-size data, you will notice that there are exactly 18 values greater than 7. This says that $18 \div 25$, or 72 percent, of the students have a sneaker size greater than size 7. However, the box plot suggests that 75 percent of the students wear sneakers larger than size 7. Why are these values slightly different?

DEVELOPING
ACTIVITY 2-8

Music Money Makers

Data Set 4: Top-Grossing Rock-'n'-Roll Tours contains information on the top-grossing US rock-'n'-roll tours for the year 1995. How can you use the calculator to find the *median*, or middle value, and the *mean*, or arithmetic average, for the data set? How could you find the median and mean without the calculator?

Investigate

Enter into list L1 of your calculator the gross earnings for the 10 groups. For example, enter 65.6 into L1 for The Eagles. Use Calculator Help 5: 1–Variable Stats to find the mean and the median.

```
1-VAR STATS
x̄=33.92
Σx=339.2
Sx=13.67510309
σx=12.9733419
MED=34.05
n=10
```

Your screen should look like the one shown here. Among other statistics, the screen shows that the mean $\bar{x}$ is 33.92 (million) and that the median (MED) is 34.05 (million).

Share

Explain how you would determine the median and the mean using only the original data values. In the case of the mean, you might find it helpful to note that Σ (summation symbol) on the screen shown above is the sum of all the data values.

Extend

Nicki said, "If a new data set is formed by changing every value in the original data to the mean, the sum of all the values in the new and original data sets will be the same."

Is Nicki correct? Justify your response.

How does Nicki's statement help you explain how to determine the mean of a data set?

DEVELOPING
ACTIVITY 2-9

Does the Average Change?

> Suppose that in Data Set 4, The Eagles' tour had grossed $40.0 million rather than $65.6 million. Would this have changed the median? Would it have changed the mean?

Investigate

Before doing any calculations, predict whether the mean, median, or both will change for the modified data set.

Be sure that the gross earnings, with 40.0 entered instead of 65.6 for The Eagles, have been entered into list L1 of your calculator. Use Calculator Help 5: 1-Variable Stats to find the median and mean for the modified data set.

Share

Was your prediction correct? Why or why not?

Why do you think one statistic changed and the other did not for the modified data set? Will this always be the case when an extreme data value is changed? Check your thinking by modifying the data further. Change Alan Jackson's earnings from 17.3 to 5.0 million and recalculate the 1-variable statistics with your calculator.

Extend

The 11 top-grossing US rock-'n'-roll tours for the year 1995 include the 10 groups shown in Data Set 4 plus Jimmy Buffet. If the inclusion of Jimmy Buffet changes the mean gross earnings from $33.92 million to $32.29 million, how much did the Jimmy Buffet tour gross in 1995?

DEVELOPING
ACTIVITY 2-10

Boxing the Top-Grossing 1995 US Tours

Construct a box plot of the 10 top-grossing 1995 US rock tours. What percentage of the data values lie between $22.8 and $36.9 million?

Investigate

Be sure that the gross earnings are entered into list L1 of your calculator. Construct a box plot for gross earnings data. What minimun, maximum, and scale values should you use for x in the window? Use Calculator Help 4: Box Plot to set the window and to define and display the box plot. You may also want to look at the box plot on your calculator and identify a number line.

Find the five-number-summary values for the data set.

Share

Which of the statistics—lower quartile, median, or upper quartile—are contained in the original data set? Why are some of these in the data set and others not?

What percentage of the data values lie between the lower quartile, $22.8 million, and the upper quartile, $36.9 million? Will this percentage be the same for the boxed part of any box plot? Explain.

The box length in any box plot is called the *interquartile range*. Explain why this is an appropriate name. How does the interquartile range, or IQR, differ from the range of a data set?

Extend

If a data value is more than 1.5 times the length of the box above the upper quartile, it is said to be an outlier. Similarly if it is more than 1.5 times the length of the box below the lower quartile it is also an outlier. Does the data set of 10 top-grossing 1995 US rock tours have any outliers?

DEVELOPING
ACTIVITY 2-11

Top-Grossing US Tours in 1995 and 1994

Data Set 4 contains information on the 10 top-grossing US rock-'n'-roll tours for the year 1994 as well as 1995. How can you use the calculator to construct box plots for both the 1994 and 1995 data on the same number scale? What do the box plots tell you about the differences between tour earnings for 1995 and 1994?

Investigate

Be sure that the gross earnings for 1995 have been entered into list L1 and the gross earnings for 1994 have been entered into list L2 of your calculator. Use Calculator Help 4: Box Plot to construct both the 1994 and the 1995 plots.

- Set XMIN and XMAX in the window to cover the range of values in both data sets. Use 0 for YMIN and 5 for YMAX.
- Use Stat Plot 1 for the 1995 data and Stat Plot 2 for the 1994 data. Both Stat Plots must be turned on.

Find the five-number-summary values for the 1995 earnings and the 1994 earnings. Also find the interquartile range for each year's earnings.

Share

What do the box plots tell you about the differences between the 1995 and 1994 earnings? It may also be helpful to examine each year's five-number-summary values and the interquartile ranges.

Extend

Which year's gross earnings do you predict will have the greater mean? Use your calculator to find the means and then check your prediction. Was your prediction correct? Why or why not?

DEVELOPING
ACTIVITY 2-12

Scoring an Ice-Skating Competition

In an ice-skating competition, Caterina and Cristie were the top two competitors. Five judges gave them the scores shown in Data Set 5: Judges' Scores for Ice-Skating Competition. Did Caterina or Cristie win the competition, or was it a tie?

Investigate

Use your calculator to determine any statistics that may be useful in determining a winner. It may also be helpful to look at the spread of the scores for each skater using the range and the interquartile range.

Share

How are the two sets of scores alike and how are they different?

Suppose you were the tournament referee. What would you decide about a winner of this competition? Justify your thinking based on your analysis of the data.

Extend

In some competitions, each competitor's highest and lowest scores are eliminated and then the mean of the remaining three scores is used to determine a winner. Who would win the competition under these conditions? Is this a fairer method? Explain.

DEVELOPING
ACTIVITY 2-13 | Box Plots and Ice-Skating Competition

> Use your calculator to construct two box plots, one for Caterina's scores and one for Cristie's scores, shown in Data Set 5. What do the box plots tell you about the two sets of scores? How are the box plots alike and how are they different?

Investigate

Be sure that Caterina's scores have been entered into list L1 and Cristie's scores have been entered into list L2 of your calculator. Use the Calculator Help 4: Box Plot to construct the two plots.

- Set the window to cover the range of values in both sets. Use 0 for YMIN and 5 for YMAX.
- Use Stat Plot 1 for Caterina's data and Stat Plot 2 for Christie's data. Both Stat Plots must be turned on.

Find the five-number-summary values and the interquartile range for each set of scores.

Share

What do the box plots tell you about the two sets of scores? How are they alike and how are they different?

Extend

Why does Caterina's box plot have no "whiskers"?

DEVELOPING
ACTIVITY 2-14

Ice-Skating Competition and Standard Deviation

The *standard deviation* is an index that measures the spread of the data set about the mean. You use the calculator to find the standard deviation for each of Caterina's and Christie's set of scores in Data Set 5. Compare the two sets of scores using the means and the standard deviations.

Investigate

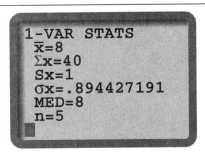

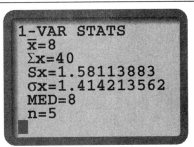

Be sure that Caterina's scores have been entered into list L1 and Cristie's scores have been entered into list L2 of your calculator. Use Calculator Help 5: 1-Variable Stats to find the standard deviation (Sx) and mean $\bar{x}$ for each set of scores. Your screens should look like the two shown here. Caterina's statistics are on the left screen and Christie's are on the right screen.

Share

Which set of scores has the greater standard deviation? If standard deviation is a measure of the spread of a data set, would you have expected this result? Explain.

How are your conclusions using means and standard deviations similar to those using medians and interquartile ranges? Explain your thinking.

Extend

Construct a data set with the same number of data values and the same mean as those of Caterina and Christie but with a standard deviation between those of Caterina and Christie.

DEVELOPING
ACTIVITY 2-15

Delving into Middle-School Basketball Data

In the Azuma Middle School Girls' Basketball Tournament, the final was between the Bluebirds and the Hawks. Some of the data for this game are given in Data Set 6: Middle-School Basketball Statistics. Which team had the most fouls? Which team won the final?

Investigate

Use your calculator to find any totals that you need to determine the team with the most fouls and the team that won the final.

Share

The information in Data Set 6 is called *three-variable data*. What makes this an appropriate description of the data?

Write a brief paragraph for a school newspaper that includes, among other information, which team won the game and which team committed the greater number of fouls.

Extension

Is it possible to determine how long the game lasted?

If it is possible, find the length of the game in minutes and explain your reasoning.

If this is not possible, explain why it cannot be done using the data provided.

Finding Relationships in Basketball Data

Is there any relationship between the total points scored and the time spent on the bench for the players listed on the Middle-School Basketball information in Data Set 6? How could you use the calculator to construct a scatter plot for the two variables: total number of points scored and time spent on the bench? What does the scatter plot tell you about the relationship between the two variables?

Investigate

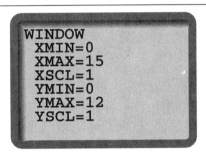

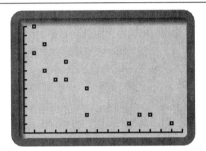

Enter into list L1 of your calculator the time spent on the bench for each of the 14 players. Enter into list L2 of your calculator the total number of points scored for each of the 14 players. Use Calculator Help 6: Scatter Plot to construct the plot.

- Set the window using the values shown here.
- Define and display the scatter plot according to the steps described in the calculator help.

Your screen should look like the one shown here.

Share

What happens to the total points scored as the time on the bench increases?

What does your scatter plot suggest about the relationship between total points scored and time on the bench for these players? Write a paragraph to describe the relationship. Be sure to talk about the shape of the scatter plot.

Extend

If the game lasted 20 minutes, find the playing time for each player.

Construct a scatter plot to investigate the relationship between total points scored and playing time in minutes for the players. What does the scatter plot tell you? How is this scatter plot similar to and also different from the scatter plot for total points scored and time spent on the bench? Explain.

DEVELOPING
ACTIVITY 2-17 # More Relationships in Basketball Data

> Is there a relationship between the total points scored and the number of fouls for the Middle-School Basketball information in Data Set 6? Construct a scatter plot for the two variables: total number of points scored and number of fouls. What does the scatter plot tell you about the relationship between the two variables?

Investigate

Enter into list L1 of your calculator the number of fouls for each of the 14 players. Enter into list L2 of your calculator the total number of points scored for each of the 14 players. Use Calculator Help 6: Scatter Plot to construct the plot.

- Set the window values. To determine XMIN, XMAX, YMIN, and YMAX, you will need to examine the range of values for fouls (x) and the range for total points (y).
- Define and display the scatter plot according to the steps described in the calculator help.

Share

What happens to the total points scored as the number of fouls increases?

What does your scatter plot suggest about the relationship between total points scored and number of fouls for these players? Write a paragraph to describe the relationship.

How does this relationship differ from the relationships you found between

- total points scored and time on the bench
- total points scored and playing time

in Finding Relationships in Basketball Data? Concentrate on the shape of each scatter plot as you compare relationships.

Extend

Construct a scatter plot to investigate the relationship between number of fouls and playing time in minutes.

- Is the scatter plot what you expected? Why or why not?
- Compare this scatter plot with the scatter plot you just constructed that showed the relationship between the total points scored and the number of fouls for each player.

APPLYING
ACTIVITY 2-18

Movie Running Times

> Data Set 7: Movie Running Times includes information on the running times for movies shown during a holiday season. What do you need to do to this data so it can be entered into your calculator for exploration?

Investigate

Which of the following are appropriate ways of expressing the running time for *Dracula: Dead and Loving It* so that it can be entered into list L1 of the TI-80?

- 1.30 hours
- 90 minutes
- 130 minutes
- 1.5 hours
- $1\frac{30}{60}$ hours

Share

Explain why 90 minutes, 1.5 hours, and $1\frac{30}{60}$ hours are appropriate ways to enter the running time for *Dracula: Dead and Loving It*. Why are the other two expressions inappropriate?

Extend

Enter into calculator list L1 the running times for all the movies, expressed in hours using decimal fractions, such as 1.5 hours for *Dracula: Dead and Loving It*. Now enter into list L2 the running times for all the movies using mixed numbers (such as $1\frac{30}{60}$ hours for *Dracula: Dead and Loving It*). Use Calculator Help 7: Entering Fractions for help with L2.

What do you notice about the data in the two lists? Explain your results.

Ordering the Movie Running Times

The movies in Data Set 7 are ordered alphabetically. How can you use your calculator to order the data set by running times? What does it mean to order the data by running times?

Investigate

Be sure the movie running times, in hours, have been entered into list L1 of your calculator. Use Calculator Help 2: Sorting Lists to order the data by running times.

Share

Describe what the sort features have done to the original data set. How are the two sort features alike and how are they different?

Extend

Is it appropriate to enter the movie running times in minutes rather than in hours and then sort the data? Explain.

Running-Times Data Patterns

> Write a letter to a friend summarizing information about the
> running times of the movies in Data Set 7.

Investigate

Examine features of the data set. Look for

- the range
- outliers
- gaps and clusters

Mention any other patterns or trends you identify in the data.

Share

What does the numerical ordering tell you about the data that may not have been apparent in the alphabetical ordering? Explain.

Write a letter to your friend summarizing the information on movie running times and share it with your classmates.

Extend

If you could watch a maximum of 6 hours of movies each day, could you see all the movies from Data Set 7 in 7 days? Is this the least number of days required? Describe your strategy for solving the problem.

APPLYING ACTIVITY 2-21

Picturing the Movie Running Times

> What does a histogram reveal about the patterns in Data Set 7?

Investigate

Be sure the movie running times, in minutes, have been entered into list L1 of your calculator.

Construct two histograms for the data, one using a class width 10 minutes and another with a class width 20 minutes. In each case, start the first class at 70. Use Calculator Help 3: Histogram to help you complete the two histograms. Define the histogram plot using Stat Plot 1 and then change XSCL in the window when producing two histograms.

Share

What does the histogram with class width 10 reveal about the data that is not as evident in the histogram with class width 20?

In what ways do the two histograms reveal similar information?

Extend

What percentage of the movies run for more than 2 hours? Show how to solve the problem in more than one way and then compare your answers.

APPLYING
ACTIVITY 2-22

Another Picture of Movie Running Times

> Use a box plot to display the Movie Running Times information in Data Set 7. What does the box plot tell you about the movie running-time data? Compare the histogram and box plot displays for the movie running-times data. Is one display more useful than the other? Why?

Investigate

Be sure the movie running times, in minutes, have been entered into list L1 of your calculator and that a histogram of the data is defined in Stat Plot 1.

Construct a box plot of the data. Use Calculator Help 4: Box Plot to create your plot. Define the box plot using Stat Plot 2. You should see the histogram and the box plot on the same screen.

Share

What information about the movie running times is revealed in the box plot?

Complete this statement.

"Fifty percent (50%) of the movies run longer than _____ minutes."

Explain how you determined this value. Which display, the box plot or the histogram, was more useful in making this determination?

Now complete this statement.

"Ninety percent (90%) of the movies run longer than _____ minutes."

Which display is now more useful? Explain.

Extend

Which display, the histogram or the box plot, is more useful for determining what percent of the movies run for more than 1 hour 50 minutes?

Justify your reasoning.

APPLYING
ACTIVITY 2-23

Do Weeks Shown Depend on Movie Running Time?

Examine the movie running time and the number of weeks shown for each of the movies presented in Data Set 7. Is the number of weeks shown related to a movie's running time? Why or why not?

Investigate

Be sure the movie running times, in minutes, have been entered into list L1 of your calculator and that the number of weeks shown has been entered into list L2.

Construct a scatter plot to show movie running times, in minutes, and the number of weeks shown. Use Calculator Help 6: Scatter Plot to construct the plot.

Share

What does the scatter plot suggest about any relationships between movie running times and the number of weeks shown?

Try to envision a straight line placed on the scatter plot that would show the relationship between running times and weeks shown. Use a piece of yarn or spaghetti placed on your calculator to show this line.

How many points on the scatter plot actually touch, or fit, your envisioned line?

Extend

The movie *The Birdcage* runs for 1 hour 59 minutes. Predict the number of weeks the movie will show. Explain how you made your prediction. You may find it helpful to use TRACE and ◀ ▶ to help identify points on your scatter plot.

Population Density of Ten US Cities

> Data Set 8: Population Density and Unemployment in 10 US Cities shows the population, area, and percentage of unemployed people for 10 cities in the Unites States. Compare and contrast the cities with respect to population overcrowding.

Investigate

Sally says, "A good way to measure population overcrowding is to divide the population by the area. This quotient is called the *population density*."

Use Sally's method to find the population density for each of the 10 cities shown in Data Set 8.

Enter the 10 populations into list L1 of your calculator and the corresponding areas into list L2. Use your calculator to compute the population density for the 10 cities.

Share

What is it about Sally's method that makes it effective for measuring population overcrowding?

Write a letter to a friend in Australia telling her what you found out about population overcrowding in these 10 US cities.

Extend

Boris suggests another method for measuring population overcrowding. He suggests subtracting the area from the population. What do you think about Boris's method?

APPLYING
ACTIVITY 2-25

Population Density and Percentage Unemployed

Is there a relationship between population density and percentage of unemployed people for the 10 cities shown in Data Set 8?

Investigate

Be sure that population density is entered into list L1 of your calculator and that the percentage unemployed is entered into list L2 of your calculator.

Use your calculator to generate appropriate numerical statistics and visual displays to describe the relationship between population density and percentage unemployed for these 10 cities.

Share

Describe the relationship you found between population density and percentage unemployed. Share your findings with your classmates. Include in your report any numerical statistics and visual displays you used.

Extend

Use the relationship you found to predict the percentage unemployed in New York City, knowing its population is 7,322,564 people and that it has an area of 301 square miles.

ACTIVITY 2-26 Sighting a Line of Best Fit

> How can you construct a straight line to fit the relationship between population density and percentage of unemployed people for Data Set 8? How good a fit is your straight line?

Investigate

Be sure that population density data (x) are entered into list L1 of your calculator and that the percentage unemployed data (y) are entered into list L2 of your calculator. Use Calculator Help 6: Scatter Plot to construct a scatter plot of the data.

With the scatter plot showing on your calculator, use Calculator Help 8: Line Drawing to draw the line that you think best fits the data, that is, the line that seems closest to as many points as possible. (You can try more than one line with the DRAW tool of the calculator.)

Share

Describe the line you have chosen as the best-fit line for the data. Include in your description reasons for your choice of a best-fit line. Share your visual display and your description with classmates.

Extend

How can you use the straight line to find the percentage unemployed in New York? How does your result compare with the result you found in the Extend to Population Density and Percentage Unemployed?

Sneakers Revisited

Mark is a new student in the class of students shown in Data Set 3. The length of Mark's sneakers is 31 centimeters. Predict Mark's sneaker size and explain how you determined it.

Investigate
Look at all of the data you have on sneakers. How can you use these data to make a prediction?

What statistics and visual displays might be helpful?

Share
Write a report that describes and explains what you did and indicates the conclusions you have drawn in predicting Mark's sneaker size.

Extend
What if the length of Mark's sneakers had been 36 cm? Could you have used the same approach? Why or why not?

CHALLENGING
ACTIVITY 2-28

Two-Phone-Line Homes on the Rise

> In the visual display shown below, it is suggested that an estimated 50 percent of all US homes will have multiple phone lines by the year 2000. How might the investigators have arrived at the figure of 50 percent?

Investigate   How could you use one or both of the lines on the graph to estimate the percentage of US homes that will have multiple phone lines by the year 2000?

Share   Describe how you made your estimate.

Was your estimate in agreement with the estimate presented in the illustration? If not, can you explain the difference?

Extension   If the data on phone lines had been available only until the end of 1994, what percentage would you have predicted for the year 2000? Explain your method.

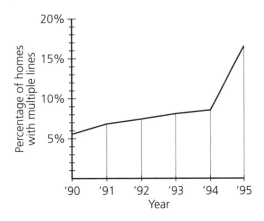

Two-Phone-Line Homes Rise

An estimated 50 percent of all US homes will have multiple phone lines by 2000 to serve home offices, modems, and so on.

Module 3

PROBABILITY

Overview

The tasks in this module focus on real-world problems involving chance. The problems can be solved by finding experimental probabilities using spinners, dice, or random-number models. They can also be solved by using theoretical probabilities. Graphics calculators such as the TI-80 not only allow students to generate appropriate sets of random numbers, but they also allow students to create visual displays of experimental results.

The expected outcomes of the Probability module are that students will be able to

- list the outcomes of single-stage and multi-stage random experiments

- collect and use appropriate data to find experimental probabilities

- use reasoning to determine theoretical probabilities

- determine experimental and theoretical conditional probabilities

- recognize pairs of independent and non-independent events

The calculator-supported activities in this module are designed to provide a rich development in experimental probability through modeling and simulation. Such experimentation is expected to facilitate students' understanding of theoretical probabilities. This development illustrates the use of an instructional sequence that begins with prediction, moves to experimentation, and culminates with analysis.

In order to provide an appropriate development of probability for middle-school students, this module has the flexibility to be used as a replacement unit or as a supplemental unit. When the module is used as a replacement unit, we suggest you help students explore consecutively as many of the Developing activities (3-1 to 3-18) as time permits. In so doing, you may find it helpful to present your own problems to focus on areas where students need additional experiences. Depending on students' background, you may need to help students explore a number of basic probability concepts as the Developing activities unfold. Some of the key concepts include random experiments, sample space, experimental probability, theoretical probability, conditional probability, and independent events. The content background section contains ideas and experiences you can easily use during instruction. This approach would allow you to use some of the Applying and the Challenging activities as projects or to use the Applying and the Challenging activities in subsequent years.

If *Module 3: Probability* serves as a supplemental unit, you could have students explore probability using the Applying activities of the module. Alternatively, students could first explore the Developing activities that incorporate key mathematical concepts that have not been adequately developed in the students' textbook. If this approach is used, the Challenging activities would make ideal projects or assessment tasks.

Use the content background (pages 97–100) for your own review of probability concepts and vocabulary. Information of presenting the student activities (pages 107–137) begins on page 101.

Outline of Key Mathematical Ideas

DEVELOPING ACTIVITIES   **KEY MATHEMATICAL IDEAS**

3-1 Flipping a Nickel	random experiments
3-2 Experimental Probability	experimental and theoretical probabilities
3-3 Rolling a Die	experimental and theoretical probabilities
3-4 Picturing the Die Data	experimental probability
3-5 The Gumball Machine	experimental and theoretical probabilities
3-6 Another Look at Gumball Probabilities	theoretical probability
3-7 Modeling the Gumball Machine	modeling probability
3-8 Another Gumball Model	models and simulation
3-9 Flipping a Nickel and a Quarter	multi-stage experiments
3-10 Nickel-and-Quarter Outcomes	sample space and simulation
3-11 Music Time	experimental and theoretical probabilities
3-12 More Music	experimental probability
3-13 Shooting Free Throws	experimental probability
3-14 Can a Coin Remember?	independent events
3-15 What's the Chance of a Red Gumball?	conditional probability
3-16 Snow on the Flower Bed	geometric probability
3-17 Rain on the Plain	geometric probability
3-18 Too Much Rain on the Plain	geometric probability

APPLYING ACTIVITIES   **KEY MATHEMATICAL IDEAS**

3-19 Steffi Versus Monica	experimental and theoretical probabilities
3-20 Summer Music Time	experimental and theoretical probabilities
3-21 Have the Chances Changed?	independent events
3-22 The Windsurfer Race	theoretical probability
3-23 Getting a Green Light	experimental and theoretical probabilities
3-24 Can You Guess the Secret Number?	conditional probability
3-25 A Tied Election	conditional probability
3-26 Extra Information in a Tied Election	conditional probability
3-27 Eva at the Free-Throw Line	conditional probability

CHALLENGING ACTIVITIES   **KEY MATHEMATICAL IDEAS**

3-28 Lucky Number Combination	conditional probability
3-29 Which Die Numbers?	expected values
3-30 Drawing For a Festival Ticket	conditional probability

Content Background

Experimental and Theoretical Probabilities

Experiments involving chance result in outcomes that normally cannot be predicted with certainty. We say such experiments are random, in the sense that their long-term behavior is predictable but their short-term behavior is not. The study of probability aims at establishing numerical values to indicate the likelihood of a particular outcome or event.

For example, the data shown in the table below present the batting record of the top five players on the Stevenson Middle School softball team.

Stevenson Middle School Softball

Player	Hits/At Bats	Batting Average
Sheryl	25/50	0.500
Barbara	24/60	0.400
Roberta	31/50	0.620
Stephanie	20/54	0.370
Wanda	18/39	0.462

To interpret these figures, we need to set the context. Suppose Sheryl is at the plate as the first batter of the game. We know her at-bat will result in one of two outcomes, or results: a hit or not a hit. Note that in softball, any outcome that is not a safe hit, such as a walk, is considered not a hit. These two outcomes are said to be the sample space for the activity of being at bat.

Based on the data available, the probability that Sheryl will make a hit is 0.500 because 50 percent of her at-bats have resulted in hits. In this case, we are using experimental probability, usually defined as

$$\frac{\text{number of successes}}{\text{number of trials}}.$$

Experimental probability is calculated from existing data as in this example or by repeating a number of trials in an experiment and noting the number of times the desired event occurs. Each time the desired event occurs counts as a success.

By way of contrast, theoretical probabilities are determined by physical characteristics, numerical composition, geometrical properties, or by other probability calculations. For example, when tossing a coin we assign a probability of 0.5 to a head and also to a tail on the basis that the coin is symmetrical, and heads and tails are equally weighted. For the same reason, each of the numbers 1 through 6 has the probability of occurring $\frac{1}{6}$ of the time when a fair die is rolled. In both of these activities, the probabilities of each outcome in the sample space are the same, hence, the outcomes are said to be equally likely.

Outcomes are not always equally likely. For example, suppose we buy a gumball from a machine that contains 12 red gumballs, 8 green gumballs, and 5 white gumballs. Assuming that the gumballs are dispensed randomly, the probability of getting a red gumball is $\frac{12}{25}$, the probability of getting a green gumball is $\frac{8}{25}$, and the probability of getting a white gumball is $\frac{5}{25}$. The reasoning for these probabilities is based on the numerical composition of the gumballs in the machine. Although getting each of the three colors is not equally likely, getting each of the 25 gumballs is equally likely.

Fundamental Properties of Experimental and Theoretical Probabilities

Both experimental probabilities and theoretical probabilities have the following properties:

- The probability of an event is a real number between 0 and 1 inclusive.

- The sum of the probabilities of all outcomes in the sample space is 1.

To illustrate, let us reconsider Barbara at the plate. Again, there are two outcomes, hit and not a hit. Because she has hit safely in $\frac{24}{60}$ attempts during the season, she must have failed to make a hit $\frac{36}{60}$ times. Her probabilities are 0.400 for a hit and 0.600 for not a hit. Both of these probabilities are between 0 and 1; and because these are the only two outcomes, the sum of the probabilities is 1. We note that the event "hit or not a hit" is certain to occur; this has the maximum allowable probability of 1. By way of contrast, it is impossible for a batter to earn a hit when a pop fly is caught, and this event has the minimum possible probability of 0.

Determining Theoretical Probability

Although the emphasis in the Probability Activities is on modeling and simulations, you will want to devote some class time to theoretical probability. The problems below illustrate a way to determine theoretical probabilities in a variety of multi-stage experiments.

Problem 1 Suppose Stephanie bats twice in the same inning. What is the probability that both at-bats will result in a hit?

Solution The probability that Stephanie makes a hit is 0.370. We signify this by P(H) = 0.370. We also note that the probability that she does not make a hit is 0.630, denoted by P(N) = 0.630. The tree diagram shown on page 98 identifies the four two-stage outcomes and their corresponding probabilities. If E is the event that Stephanie hits safely both times, E = {(H, H)}, and P(E) = 0.137.

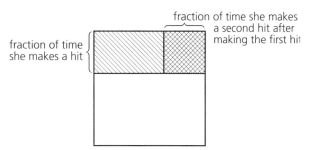

This can also be understood through percentages. Thirty-seven percent of the time she makes the first hit and 37% of that 37%, she makes a second hit as well. That is 37% of 37% or 0.37×0.37, which is 0.137. This is illustrated in the area diagram.

```
                              fraction of time she makes
                              a second hit after
                              making the first hit
fraction of time {
she makes a hit
```

Problem 2 In the last inning of a game, the coach allows a player to bat twice only if the first at-bat results in a hit. Under these circumstances, what is the probability that Stephanie will have at least one hit in the last inning?

P(H) = 0.370 H
P(H) = 0.370 H (H, H) P(H, H) = (0.370) × (0.370) = 0.137
P(N) = 0.630 N (H, N) P(H, N) = (0.370) × (0.630) = 0.233
P(N) = 0.630 N ———— (N, –) P(N, –) = 0.630

Solution The tree diagram above shows the three outcomes and their associated probabilities. Note that when Stephanie does not make a hit on the first at-bat, there is no second at-bat. As a result, the set of outcomes in this sample space is {(H, H), (H, N), (N, –)} where the dash indicates there was no second at-bat. While the outcomes are not all two-stage outcomes, the tree diagram shows that the sum of the probabilities is equal to 1.

Let D be the event that Stephanie makes at least one hit. Then D = {(H, H), (H, N)}, and P(D) = 0.370.

Note: In solving Problems 1 and 2, we assume that all events are independent; that is, the result of Stephanie's second at-bat is independent of the outcome of her first at-bat. In essence, this means that the probability Stephanie makes a hit does not change.

Problem 3 Wanda buys two gumballs from a gumball machine that contains 12 red gumballs and 8 green gumballs. Assuming that the gumballs are dispensed randomly, what is the probability that Wanda will get one red gumball and one green gumball?

Solution The probability that Wanda will get a red gumball on her first try is $\frac{12}{20}$, and the probability that she will get a green gumball on the first try is $\frac{8}{20}$. If she gets a red gumball first, the probability of her getting a red gumball on the second try will change to $\frac{11}{19}$ and the probability of her getting a green gumball will now be $\frac{8}{19}$. If, however, she gets a green gumball first, the probability of her getting a red gumball on the second try will change to $\frac{12}{19}$ and the probability of her getting a green gumball will be $\frac{7}{19}$.

P(R) = $\frac{12}{20}$ R
    P(R) = $\frac{11}{19}$ R (R, R)
    P(G) = $\frac{8}{19}$ G (R, G)
P(G) = $\frac{8}{20}$ G
    P(R) = $\frac{12}{19}$ R (G, R)
    P(G) = $\frac{7}{19}$ G (G, G)

The probabilities associated with Wanda's second gumball are all conditional probabilities, because they depend on the result of her first try. Notice that the gumballs are not replaced in this situation.

If A is the event that Wanda gets one gumball of each color, then A = {(G, R), (R, G)}, and P(A) = 0.506.

An easier example of conditional probability is this situation: A die is rolled and you are told that an even number has come up. What is the probability that it is a 6? In this case, the conditional probability is $\frac{1}{3}$, because the sample space has been reduced to the three outcomes 2, 4, 6. Compare this to the probability of rolling a 6 with no conditions imposed. See the glossary for a definition as well.

Simulation Simulations are used extensively in science, commerce, sports, and other situations to estimate probabilities. Because the long-term experimental probability approximates the theoretical probability, simulation can be used to solve problems where theoretical probabilities are difficult or impossible to determine.

In Problems 4 through 6, we demonstrate the simulation process using random numbers generated with a TI-80 graphics calculator.

Problem 4 Use random numbers to simulate 5 at-bats by Barbara. How many times in 5 at-bats does she make a hit?

Solution Simulation Sequence for Problem 4

Step 1—Model There are only two outcomes, hit and not a hit. Because the probability that Barbara will make a hit is 0.4, the probability that she will not make a hit is 0.6.

Use **RANDINT(** on the TI-80 to model Barbara's at-bats. Press [MATH] and use the right arrow key [▶] to go to **PRB**. Now press [5]. You should see **RANDINT(** on your screen. Then enter **1,10)** and press [ENTER]. This will generate random integers from 1 to 10, inclusive. To model Barbara's at-bats, use the integers 1, 2, 3, 4 to represent a hit and the integers 5, 6, 7, 8, 9, 10 to represent that Barbara did not make a hit. This assignment insures that P(H) = 0.4 and P(N) = 0.6. Other assignments of four and six integers, respectively, could be used to insure that these probabilities apply.

Step 2—Trial A trial consists of generating a random integer and noting whether it is in the set 1 through 4, for a hit, or 5 through 10, for not a hit.

Step 3—Repeat Five trials are required to simulate five at-bats.

Step 4—Record the Outcomes Five single-digit random numbers from a TI-80 calculator are shown.

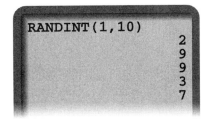

Step 5 Summarize and Draw Conclusions In the five random numbers, there are two in the set 1 through 4 and three in the set 5 through 10. In these five at-bats, Barbara will hit safely twice and will not make a hit on the other three at-bats.

Notes

1. With probabilities given in tenths, it was possible to model with single-digit random numbers.
   What if Roberta had been at the plate? Her probability of getting a hit is 0.62, or $\frac{31}{50}$. To model Roberta's at-bats, you might use either **RANDINT(1,100)** or **RANDINT(1,50)**. In the first case, the integers 1 through 62 represent a hit and the integers 63 through 100 represent no hit. In the second case, the integers 1 through 31 represent a hit and the integers 32 through 50 represent not a hit. These are equivalent.

2. Barbara's at-bats can be modeled in other ways. For example, you can use a spinner, like the one shown here, or a pack of ten cards with four of them labeled hit and six of them labeled not a hit.

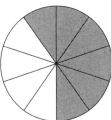

Problem 5 Stephanie bats twice during a game. What is the probability that both at-bats will result in a hit?

Solution Simulation Sequence for Problem 5

Step 1—Model As before, there are only two outcomes for each at-bat, hit and not a hit. Since the probability that Stephanie will make a hit is 0.37, the probability that she will not make a hit is 0.63.

Use **RANDINT(** on the TI-80 to model Stephanie's at-bats. Press [MATH] and use the right arrow key [▶] to go to **PRB**. Now press [5]. You should see **RANDINT(** on your screen. Then enter **1,100)** and press [ENTER]. This will generate random integers from 1 to 100, inclusive. To model Stephanie's at-bats, use the integers 1 through 37 to represent a hit and the integers 38 through 100 to represent not make a hit. This assignment insures that P(H) = 0.37 and P(N) = 0.63.

Step 2—Trial Because Stephanie bats twice in a game, one trial consists of generating a pair of random integers and noting whether or not both are in the set 1 through 37.

Step 3—Repeat We will use 30 trials from which the experimental probability can be determined.

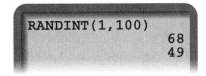

Step 4—Record the Outcomes We are interested in successes (Stephanie will get two hits in two at-bats) and non-successes (Stephanie will get fewer than two hits in two at-bats). Record whether or not each trial is a success. The screen shows the two random numbers that constitute the first trial. Because both values are greater than 37, Stephanie did not get two hits in this trial, that is, in two at-bats.

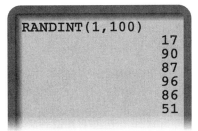

Step 5—Summarize and Draw Conclusions The TI-80 screen shows three more trials. On none of these did Stephanie get two hits.

When we completed the 30 trials, Stephanie had 3 successes and 27 non-successes. This results in the experimental probability of making two hits $\frac{3}{30} = 0.1$.

Notes

1. Using a tree diagram, the theoretical probability that Stephanie makes two hits in two at-bats is $(0.37)^2 = 0.14$. This assumes that each at-bat is an independent event.

2. It is important to note that each trial comprises two random integers 1 through 100.

Problem 6 Joyce is another member of the Stevenson Middle School softball team. She has an interesting at-bat record. If she makes a hit in an at-bat, the probability she will make a hit in the next at-bat is 0.3. If she fails to make a hit, the probability that she will not make a hit on the next at-bat is 0.8.

Carry out a simulation to determine the mean number of hits Joyce will make in a game where she bats three times. Assume that on Joyce's first at-bat of a game, her probability of getting a hit is 0.3.

Solution Simulation Sequence for Problem 6

Step 1—Model Use the notation $P(H \mid H)$ to represent the probability of making a hit on the next at-bat, given that she just made a hit and use $P(N \mid N)$ to represent the probability of not making a hit given that she just failed to make a hit. From the problem statement, we have $P(H \mid H) = 0.3$ and $P(N \mid N) = 0.8$. Given that a hit was made on the first at bat, "hit" and "no hit" are complements on the next at bat. See also the glossary for a definition of complementary events. Using complements, we can determine $P(N \mid H)$, the probability of not making a hit, given that Joyce made a hit on the previous at-bat, and $P(H \mid N)$, the probability of making a hit given that she did not make a hit on the previous at bat. We have $P(N \mid H) = 1 - 0.3 = 0.7$ and $P(H \mid N) = 1 - 0.8 = 0.2$.

We can use random numbers from 1 through 10 to model Joyce's at-bats, as shown in the table below.

Random-Number Assignment	Joyce will make a hit on her next at-bat.	Joyce will not make a hit on her next at-bat.
Joyce made a hit.	1 2 3	4 5 6 7 8 9 10
Joyce did not make a hit.	1 2	3 4 5 6 7 8 9 10

Step 2—Trial A trial consists of generating three random integers. Each trial must be modeled according to

the outcome of the previous trial and the random number assignment described in the table above. Note that on each game's first at-bat, the assignment is the same as if Joyce had just made a hit.

Step 3—Repeat We need a number of trials from which we can determine the desired mean value. We will consider the results from 10 trials.

Step 4—Record the Outcomes We are interested in the number of hits made in three at-bats. For each trial, or game, record the number of hits.

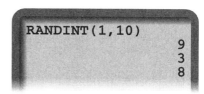

Step 5—Summarize and Draw Conclusions A TI-80 screen shows the results of one trial. On the first at-bat, Joyce failed to make a hit (9). On the second at-bat, Joyce failed to make a hit (3). On the third at-bat, she failed once again to make a hit (8). In this trial, Joyce made 0 hits.

Here are the random numbers associated with 10 trials.

9 3 8	1 6 3	3 2 5	5 1 2	3 5 5
2 1 7	1 6 4	3 6 1	10 10 4	5 5 1

Here are the number of hits for each trial.

0	1	2	2	1
2	1	2	0	1

The mean number of hits is 1.2, as 12 hits were made in 10 games.

Notes

1. The assignment of random numbers must be in accord with each conditional probability. For example, the assignment for $P(H \mid H)$ is different from $P(H \mid N)$.

2. The result of each trial must be carefully recorded. Each outcome that is part of a trial, and the relevant probability of that outcome, depends on the previous outcome.

3. The theoretical value for the mean number of hits per three at bats is 0.753 hits, so that our simulated value appears rather high.

Implementation Notes and Solutions

Developing Activities

ACTIVITY 3-1 (p. 107) RANDOM EXPERIMENTS

Flipping a Nickel

It is likely that students will predict that heads will come up 50 percent of the time, since the only two possible outcomes are heads and tails; but they will find that their group experimental results will not always show this. This would be a valuable time for you to talk with students about random processes, that is, processes whose long-term behavior is predictable but whose short-term behavior is not. It would also be helpful to contrast random behavior with chaotic behavior, in which neither short-term nor long-term behavior is predictable. The combined class data should be more representative of long-term behavior; hence, the experimental probability of heads should tend toward 0.5, its theoretical probability. The probability of getting a head is not changed by facing the head up or head down before each toss is made. There are some people who claim to be able to control the toss of a coin; but if this were the case, the process would be regulated rather than random.

ACTIVITY 3-2 (p. 108) EXPERIMENTAL AND THEORETICAL PROBABILITIES

Experimental Probability

If the class has not already discussed experimental and theoretical probability, this activity provides a good catalyst for such a discussion (refer to pages 97–98 for further information). As discussed in Activity 3-1, the experimental probability for the class data is more likely to tend toward 0.5 than each small-group experimental probability. For the Extend, both results are correct but they represent different probabilities. Joe's class data represent the experimental probability, while Aeko is talking about the theoretical probability.

ACTIVITY 3-3 (p. 109) EXPERIMENTAL AND THEORETICAL PROBABILITIES

Rolling a Die

Because it involves a different random setting, this activity provides a useful opportunity to see whether students have grasped the key ideas about experimental and theoretical probability and their relationship. It also enables you to introduce the concepts of sample space and event (refer to page 97). Although the theoretical probability of getting a 6 is $\frac{1}{6}$, the experimental probabilities of the groups might vary

substantially from this. Students should realize that the greater the number of trials, the closer the experimental probability will approximate the theoretical probability. In the Extend, the situation parallels the Extend in Activity 3-2.

ACTIVITY 3-4 (p. 110) EXPERIMENTAL PROBABILITY

Picturing the Die Data

The histogram illustrates why an average of several groups is more likely to produce a better probability estimate than the results of an individual group. This truly shows the variation in experimental probabilities. The histogram for the die data from Ms. Feeney's class is shown here, together with the window dimensions used to create the plot. The screen showing 1-variable statistics is also provided here.

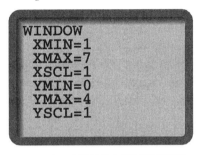

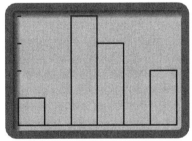

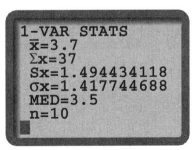

The histogram suggests that 3 lies near the center of the histogram, and that, on the average, about 3 of 30 tosses produce a 6. That is, the experimental probability is approximately 0.1. With the mean of 3.7, we get an experimental probability of $\frac{3.7}{30}$, or 0.123. This is closer to the theoretical probability of 0.17. The median of 3.5 yields an experimental probability of 0.117, marginally lower than the experimental probability using the mean. The Extend provides for your students a similar experience to the one engaged in by Ms. Feeney's class.

ACTIVITY 3-5 (p. 111) EXPERIMENTAL AND THEORETICAL PROBABILITIES

The Gumball Machine

You are most likely to get a blue gumball because its theoretical probability is 0.6 compared with 0.3 and 0.1 for the red and green gumballs, respectively. You may need to discuss this kind of simulation in some detail. It is especially important for students to realize that a ball must be replaced after each draw because it is the initial condition in the gumball machine that we are trying to simulate. Experimental probabilities will vary, but the combined class data should produce probabilities closer to the theoretical probabilities. For the Extend, students should realize that the experimental probability based on the class data should tend towards $\frac{6}{10}$, or 0.6. The more trials conducted, the better the approximation.

ACTIVITY 3-6 (p. 112) THEORETICAL PROBABILITY

Another Look at Gumball Probabilities

This activity requires students to find theoretical probabilities. In this case, the theoretical probabilities are based on the composition of the gumball machine. Because 6 of 10 gumballs are blue, the probability of blue will be $\frac{6}{10}$. Similar reasoning can be used to show that the probabilities of red and green are $\frac{3}{10}$ and $\frac{1}{10}$, respectively. In relation to Jennifer's claim, although there are only three colors, they are not equally likely because of the varying numbers of gumballs of each color. In the Extend, the probability of blue has changed for the second draw because there will be 5 blue and only 9 gumballs in all. Hence the probability of blue for the second draw will be $\frac{5}{9}$. The probability of green for the second draw is $\frac{1}{9}$, indicating that its chance of being drawn has improved slightly. The Extend is intended for students to begin thinking about conditional probability.

ACTIVITY 3-7 (p. 113) MODELING PROBABILITIES

Modeling the Gumball Machine

Several spinners are possible, but in each case the probabilities for blue, red, and green must be $\frac{6}{10}$, $\frac{3}{10}$, and $\frac{1}{10}$, respectively. For example, Claire's spinner clearly models the gumball machine, but not all the sectors belonging to a particular color are contiguous, or adjacent to one another. Some students will have difficulty with the concept of contiguous and noncontiguous outcomes in spinners, so it would be an

excellent opportunity for you to have students discuss events. It is important that students realize that an event is the set of all outcomes corresponding to a particular designation, in this case color. The Extend involves a without-replacement situation, so that the spinner will not continue to model the changing composition of the gumball machine. Of course, some students may suggest modifying the spinner, and this can be achieved by omitting appropriate sectors.

ACTIVITY 3-8 (p. 114) MODELS AND SIMULATIONS

Another Gumball Model

The process for simulating the gumball machine using the TI-80 to generate random numbers is explained in this activity. In the Extend, Pam's method is one of many ways to model the gumball machine using random numbers generated from the set 1 through 10. Any set that designates 1 number for green, 3 numbers for red, and 6 numbers for blue out of the 10 numbers will model the gumball machine.

ACTIVITY 3-9 (p. 115) MULTI-STAGE EXPERIMENTS

Flipping a Nickel and a Quarter

In this activity, we begin to look at probability situations with multiple outcomes, for example, tossing two coins. This would be an appropriate time to review sample space and to help students find systematic ways to list the outcomes of multi-stage experiments. Tree diagrams are especially helpful (refer to page 98 for further information). For the experiment of flipping a nickel and a quarter at the same time, the sample space comprises the following outcomes: (head, head), (head, tail), (tail, head), and (tail, tail), where the first outcome is associated with the flip of the nickel and the second with the flip of the quarter. Some students will have difficulty seeing that (head, tail) and (tail, head) are different outcomes. Therefore, it is crucial that they either use coins to illustrate the outcomes or that they draw them. Because both coins are symmetrical, all of the four outcomes are equally likely and hence the theoretical probability of getting heads on both is $\frac{1}{4}$. Once again the experimental probabilities of the individual groups may differ from $\frac{1}{4}$, but the probability based on the combined class data should tend toward $\frac{1}{4}$.

In the case of the Extend, tossing one coin twice is the same as tossing two different coins. This can best be explained by showing that the set of possible outcomes for the two situations is the same. Students might also recognize that the toss of the coin is not influenced by the results of a previous toss. The probability of heads remains $\frac{1}{2}$.

ACTIVITY 3-10 (p. 116)   SMAPLE SPACE AND SIMULATION

Nickel-and-Quarter Outcomes

This activity builds on Activity 3-9: Flipping a Nickel and a Quarter with respect to identifying the set of possible outcomes. In Pam's case, the theoretical probability of each outcome is $\frac{1}{4}$, but in Marion's case HT must be assigned a probability of $\frac{1}{2}$ because it represents HT and TH. Pam's set of outcomes is equally likely but Marion's is not. The combined class data from the random-number simulation should produce experimental probabilities that clarify the differences between Pam's and Marion's lists of outcomes. For Tim's double toss, a set of equally likely outcomes is (H, H), (H, T), (T, H), and (T, T). However, the probability of one of each is $\frac{1}{2}$ because either (H, T) or (T, H) causes the event to occur.

ACTIVITY 3-11 (p. 117)   EXPERIMENTAL AND THEORETICAL PROBABILITIES

Music Time

In this type of exploration, we suggest that you have students predict, experiment, and analyze. It is important to not move too quickly to a discussion of theoretical probabilities, as students may not be ready. Further simulation is a valuable tool for solving complex problems, and students will need time to learn how to construct probability models and generate simulations. The experimental probability for music both times, produced from the combined class data, should tend toward $\frac{1}{4}$ or 25 percent. In the Extend, Charles's explanation is correct because tossing two heads corresponds to music both times. The two probability models are equivalent.

ACTIVITY 3-12 (p. 118)   EXPERIMENTAL PROBABILITY

More Music

Because MUSO devotes $\frac{2}{3}$ of its air time to teen music, the probability that you will hear music continues to be $\frac{2}{3}$, assuming random tuning in to the radio station. Once again students should proceed to predict, experiment, and analyze. In fact, students may not be ready to determine the theoretical probability in this activity, and there is no need to push that at this stage. For the Extend, there are several answers. A spinner with two colors, such as red and green in the ratio 2:1, could be spun twice to model turning the radio on at two random times. Another possibility is to roll one die twice, with numbers 1 through 4 representing teen music and 5 and 6 representing not teen music.

ACTIVITY 3-13 (p. 119)   EXPERIMENTAL PROBABILITY

Shooting Free Throws

The values 1 through 10 represent one set of numbers to simulate Roger's free throws, with 1 through 6 representing a make and 7 through 10 representing a miss. A variation for the same set is to have 1 through 4 represent a miss and 5 through 10 represent a make. The experimental probability should tend toward 36 percent. In the Extend, the experimental probability of Roger scoring 1 point in a one-and-one situation should tend toward 24 percent. Note here that there is exactly one possibility for success: He must make the first and miss the second to register exactly 1 point.

ACTIVITY 3-14 (p. 120)   INDEPENDENT EVENTS

Can a Coin Remember?

This activity introduces the concept of independence. Some students, like Anna will believe that the coin must adopt its long-term behavior even in the short term. In other words, such students believe that the coin has a memory and will balance things out even in short-term sequences. This activity allows them to explore the concept and to share ideas with others. To simulate the situation, students need to keep tossing a coin and recording the outcome after each toss. From their records, they can determine the number of heads and the number of tails that followed each head. They ought to find results that tend toward an equal number of heads and tails after each head. In essence, independent events are events that do not influence each other and do not change each other's probabilities. For the Extend, all of the sequences of four outcomes are equally likely; that is, they all have a probability of $\frac{1}{16}$.

ACTIVITY 3-15 (p. 121)   CONDITIONAL PROBABILITY

What's the Chance of a Red Gumball?

This activity can be used to launch the concept of conditional probability (see page 98). The explicit nature of the gumball machine should help students see that there will only be 4 gumballs left after the first green one is drawn. Moreover, the composition will then be 3 red and 1 green gumball. This means that the conditional probability of getting red, given a green the first time, will be $\frac{3}{4}$. Similarly, the conditional probability of getting green, given a green the first time, will be $\frac{1}{4}$. Hence, both probabilities have changed for the second draw. Expressing the situation in symbols, we write P(R | G) to designate the conditional probability of Red, given Green. Notice that the events Red and Green are not independent, because drawing a green does influence the probability of red on the next draw. Contrast this with the situation confronting Anna and Tim in Activity 3-14: Can a Coin Remember?, where the events are independent. Mike's misconception in the Extend is not uncommon. She has not recognized that there are fewer gumballs left (4 rather than 5), so the probability is $\frac{3}{4}$ (0.75) rather than $\frac{3}{5}$ (0.6). In discussing Mike's problem, some students will effectively use the notion that there are "less against the red now" to mean that the complement, or the outcomes which are not in the set of given outcomes, is less.

ACTIVITY 3-16 (p. 122) GEOMETRIC PROBABILITY

Snow on the Flower Bed

Activities 3-16 through 3-18 introduce the concept of geometric probability. In geometric probability, we use measures of length, area, or volume rather than numbers to characterize the sample space and the events of a random situation. Throughout Activity 3-16, there is an assumption that Madi is watching only the snowflakes that land in the area in front of her house. Consequently, the sample space is the set of points for that area, and an appropriate measure for the sample space is area. The area measure is also appropriate for the set of points on the flower bed and on the driveway. Hence the probability that a snowflake will land in the flower bed is $\frac{6 \times 6}{75 \times 40}$ = 0.012, or 1.2 percent. Similarly, the probability that a snowflake will land on the drive way is $\frac{10 \times 40}{75 \times 40}$ = 0.1333 . . ., or about 13.3 percent. For the Extend, the probability that the next snowflake will not land on the grass is the probability that it will land on either the flower bed or the driveway which is 0.14533 . . ., or about 14.5 percent. Notice that the probability that a snowflake will land on a specific region is not influenced by the previous outcome, so the events are independent.

ACTIVITY 3-17 (p. 123) GEOMETRIC PROBABILITY

Rain on the Plain

This activity shows how to use geometric probability to solve problems involving multi-stage experiments. The probability of having rain on both days is 0.25. Several problems like this have been explored in earlier activities. They have been solved using simulation to generate an experimental probability or used mathematical reasoning to generate a theoretical probability. Wanda's square can be used again in the Extend, but the divisions would be 4:6 along one side and 6:4 along the other. This will give a desired probability of $\frac{0.4 \times 0.6}{1 \times 1}$ = 0.24.

ACTIVITY 3-18 (p. 124) GEOMETRIC PROBABILITY

Too Much Rain on the Plain

The sample space for this problem comprises the set of points on the road from Wallaby to Des Plaines. For Cindy and her dad to be past the delay zone they must be within 15 miles of Des Plaines. Using length as the appropriate measure, the probability that Cindy and her dad are past the delay zone is $\frac{15}{60}$ = 0.25. For the Extend, the probability that Cindy and her dad will be outside the delay zone when flooding occurs is $\frac{50}{60}$ = 0.833 . . . . Students might discuss why it is necessary to assume that Cindy and her dad drive at a constant speed in solving this problem.

Applying Activities

ACTIVITY 3-19 (p. 125) EXPERIMENTAL AND THEORETICAL PROBABILITIES

Steffi Versus Monica

Using the information provided, we know that in head-to-head matches between Steffi Graf and Monica Seles, Graf has won 7 out of 11 and Seles has won 4 out of 11. Based on these data, Graf is more likely to win because her probability of winning is $\frac{7}{11}$ compared with $\frac{4}{11}$ for Seles. For the Extend, more than one response is possible. Some students may claim that each match is independent, and that $\frac{7}{11}$ is the appropriate probability. While independence is tenable, some sports casters might claim that the most recent matches between the two are better indicators. Under this assumption, you could claim that Graf's probability of winning the next match is $\frac{2}{3}$, basing such a probability on only the last three matches.

ACTIVITY 3-20 (p. 126) EXPERIMENTAL AND THEORETICAL PROBABILITIES

Summer Music Time

With either simulation or an analysis based on theoretical or geometrical probability, the probability of music both times is 0.80^2 = 0.64. If the class has not considered the tree diagram-approach to multi-stage experiments (refer to pages 97–98 for further information), it could be introduced with this task.

ACTIVITY 3-21 (p. 127) INDEPENDENT EVENTS

Have the Chances Changed?

Jody is correct. The two rolls of the die are independent, so the probability of getting a 6 is not changed by the previous outcome. To set up an appropriate experiment, see the implementation notes for Activity 3-14. For the Extend, all sequences of four outcomes are equally likely. Each has a probability of $\frac{1}{1296}$.

ACTIVITY 3-22 (p. 128)   THEORETICAL PROBABILITY

The Windsurfer Race

This activity presents an excellent review of the concepts of sample space and events. While there are eleven possible outcome in terms of windsurfer numbers, these outcomes are not equally likely. For example, Windsurfer 7 has a probability of $\frac{1}{6}$ because a 7 can occur with 6 of 36 possible rolls of the two dice, namely, (1, 6), (6, 1), (2, 5), (5, 2), (3, 4), and (4, 3). Windsurfer 2, on the other hand, has a probability of $\frac{1}{36}$ because a 2 can occur only with the outcome (1, 1). Windsurfer 7 has the best chance of winning, with Windsurfers 6 and 8 the next most likely winners. For the Extend, the windsurfers are numbered 1, 2, 3, 4, 5, 6, 8, 9, 10, 12, 15, 16, 18, 20, 24, 25, 30, and 36. Using reasoning similar to that in the initial windsurfer problem, it can be shown that Windsurfers 6 and 12 have the best chance, each with $\frac{4}{36}$ as the probability of winning.

ACTIVITY 3-23 (p. 129)   EXPERIMENTAL AND THEORETICAL PROBABILITIES

Getting a Green Light

With either simulation or an analysis based on theoretical or geometrical probability, the probability that all three lights will green is $(0.4)^3 = 0.064$. This is an example in which a cube can be drawn and volume can be used in a geometric-probability approach. For the Extend, at least two green lights means two or three, that is, greater than or equal to two. Because two green lights could happen in three ways (G, G, N), (G, N, G), or (N, G, N), the probability of getting two green is $3 \times (0.4)^2 \times (0.60) = 0.29$. Hence the probability of getting at least two green lights is $0.064 + 0.288 = 0.35$.

ACTIVITY 3-24 (p. 130)   CONDITIONAL PROBABILITY

Can You Guess the Secret Number?

Because there are four letters and each has an equal chance of being the winner, the probability that Chandra will win on the first draw is $\frac{1}{4}$. On the second guess, Chandra will eliminate F, so her chance has now improved to $\frac{1}{3}$. The probability of her winning the second time is a conditional probability. Answers to the Extend will vary. One example is: The secret letter is one of the letters A, B, C, . . ., T. What is the probability that someone will guess the secret letter on the first try? ($\frac{1}{20}$) What is the probability of guessing the secret letter if you have been wrong the first two times?

($\frac{1}{18}$) What is the probability of guessing the secret letter on the second try if the secret letter is changed by random selection after each guess? ($\frac{1}{20}$)

ACTIVITY 3-25 (p. 131)   CONDITIONAL PROBABILITY

A Tied Election

Because there are four names in the bag, each with an equal chance of being drawn, the probability that Anna will win is $\frac{1}{4}$. In the second part, there are only three names in the hat for assistant captain; so the probability of Anna's name being drawn is $\frac{1}{3}$. For the Extend, three names, Jason, Tim, and Anna, will be left in the bag after Julie has been chosen captain. This means that the probability that a boy will be chosen assistant captain is $\frac{2}{3}$, compared with $\frac{2}{4}$, the probability that a boy will be chosen captain.

ACTIVITY 3-26 (p. 132)   CONDITIONAL PROBABILITY

Extra Information in a Tied Election

The task in Activity 3-26 is a nice example of a more implicit use of conditional probability. Initially, the probability of Susan winning is $\frac{1}{5}$. However, the probability of Susan winning, given that a girl's name has been drawn, is $\frac{1}{3}$ because the sample space has been reduced to the three girls, Gabriella, Angela, and Susan. For the Extend, the probability of Brett's name being drawn, given that a boy's name has been drawn, is $\frac{1}{2}$, a considerable improvement on the initial probability of $\frac{1}{5}$.

ACTIVITY 3-27 (p. 133)   CONDITIONAL PROBABILITY

Eva at the Free-Throw Line

Before asking students to explore this activity, it would be helpful to review the concept of complementary events especially in relation to conditional-probability situations. All of the outcomes in the sample space are in an event A or in its complement A prime; that is, $P(A') = 1 - P(A)$. With either simulation or an analysis based on theoretical or geometrical probability, the probability that Eva will make both free throws is $0.5 \times 0.6 = 0.3$. In the Extend, the probability that Jody will miss the first shot is $1 - 0.70 = 0.30$. The conditional probability that she will miss the second shot, given that she misses the first, is $1 - 0.90 = 0.10$. With either simulation or an analysis based on theoretical or geometrical probability, the probability that Jody will miss both free throws is $0.30 \times 0.10 = 0.03$. In the second part of the Extend, you cannot solve the problem because you do not know the conditional probability that Jody will make the second shot if she makes the first.

Challenging Activities

ACTIVITY 3-28 (p. 134) CONDITIONAL PROBABILITY

Lucky Number Combination

This task requires students to carefully list the sample space. This can be done with a tree diagram or a systematic listing of the number combinations. The task also uses the notion of complement in relating to winning and not winning. You have a better chance of not winning because the probability of not winning is $\frac{7}{8}$ compared with $\frac{1}{8}$ for winning. The second part requires a conditional probability. The probability of winning, given that your first choice was correct, is $\frac{1}{4}$. As might be expected, getting the first number correct has improved your chances. For the Extend, the probability of winning the Super Prize is $\frac{1}{16}$. If you have guessed the first two numbers correctly, the probability of winning increases to $\frac{1}{4}$.

ACTIVITY 3-29 (p. 135) EXPECTED VALUES

Which Die Numbers?

This problem introduces the notion of expected value, or weighted average, but it is not necessary to introduce expected value in a formal way as the following discussion shows. What students need to realize is that they must consider both the probability of an outcome and its score value. This is what Zach does in his solution. He is really saying that $\frac{1}{6}$ of the time Helen gets 5 points, $\frac{1}{6}$ of the time she gets 6

points, and $\frac{4}{6}$ of the time she gets 0 points. In the long run, she expects to get 11 points every six rolls of the die. Similarly, it can be shown that Simon expects, on the average, to get 10 points every six rolls of the die. Hence the game is not fair, and Helen has a better chance of winning. The Extend can be solved in a similar manner. In the long run, for every eight rolls of the die, Helen can expect to get $8 + 7 = 15$ points, and Simon can expect to get $1 + 2 + 3 + 4 + 5 = 15$ points. Hence the game is fair.

ACTIVITY 3-30 (p. 136) CONDITIONAL PROBABILITY

Drawing for a Festival Ticket

This activity makes a useful project, as students will need to recognize that it involves conditional probability. We are told that Jenny Osborne is the winner, so the question really becomes, "What is the probability that the student will be in the seventh grade, given that a girl's name has been drawn?" Because there are 52 girls in the school and only 31 of them are in the seventh grade, the required conditional probability is $\frac{31}{52} \approx 0.596$. For the Extend, Cindy's mistake did make a difference. The probability that Jenny Osborne won the family pass, given that a seventh grader was selected, is $\frac{1}{53} \approx 0.019$, which is considerably less than the earlier value of 0.596. As in all probability situations, it is vital that students determine the *sample space*, or list of the possible outcomes. In addition, for conditional probability problems, they must determine the reduced sample space.

Flipping a Nickel

If you flip a nickel, how often do you predict that it will come up heads?

Investigate

List the possible outcomes of the coin flip. If a nickel is tossed 30 times, how often do you predict that it will land heads?

Toss a nickel 30 times, record the outcome of each toss, and check your results against your prediction.

Share

Report to the rest of the class on your prediction and your experiment. Combine all of the data reported by your classmates. How often did heads come up for the entire class? Would you have predicted this? Why?

Extend

What if you always start with the head facing up when you flip the nickel? Would this change the probability of getting a head? Why or why not?

DEVELOPING ACTIVITY 3-2

Experimental Probability

Cindy says that the fraction $\dfrac{\text{number of heads}}{\text{total number of tosses}}$ is called the probability of getting a head. What was the probability of getting a head using the combined class data from the Activity 3-1: Flipping a Nickel?

Investigate

Be sure you have available the combined class data from the Activity 3-1: Flipping a Nickel. Use it to calculate the probability of getting a head using Cindy's method.

Share

Compare the probability of getting a head using the combined class data with the probability of getting a head using the data from your own 30-toss experiment. Are the probabilities different? Can you explain this?

Extend

Joe's class did the same experiment. Their class results showed that the probability of getting a head was $\frac{141}{300}$. However, Aeko says that everyone knows that the probability of getting a head is $\frac{1}{2}$, because a nickel is balanced. Who is right? Explain.

DEVELOPING
ACTIVITY 3-3

Rolling a Die

In a board game, you get bonus points for rolling a 6 with a die. What do you predict is the probability of getting a 6 on the roll of a die?

Investigate

List the possible outcomes for the roll of a die. If a die is tossed 30 times, how often do you predict that it will come up 6? Role a die 30 times to check your prediction.

Share

Report to the rest of the class on your prediction and your experiment. Combine all of the data reported by your classmates. How often did a 6 come up for the entire class? Would you have predicted this? Why?

What does this tell you about the probability of rolling a 6?

Which probability is more accurate, the combined class probability or the probability for your own 30-roll experiment? Explain.

Extend

Jane's class did the same experiment. Their class results showed that the probability of rolling a 6 was $\frac{53}{300}$. However, Boris insists that the probability of rolling a 6 is $\frac{1}{6}$ because a die has six symmetrical faces. Who is right? Explain.

Picturing the Die Data

The table below shows the experimental results from the Rolling a Die activity for Ms. Feeney's class. It shows the number of 6s in 30 tosses for each of 10 groups. Use the calculator to construct a histogram of the data for Ms. Feeney's class. What does the histogram tell you about the probability of rolling a 6?

Investigate

Number of 6s in 30 Tosses for Each of 10 Student Groups

3	6	4	3	4	3	3	4	1	6

- Create a histogram of number of 6s tossed for the student groups. Enter the number of 6s for each group into list L1 of your calculator. Set appropriate window values. Define and display the histogram according to the steps described on Calculator Help 3: Histogram.
- Use your calculator to find the mean and the median for the number-of-6s data following the steps in Calculator Help 5: 1–Variable Stats.

Share

What does the histogram tell you about the number of 6s rolled by Ms. Feeney's groups? Would you have predicted this kind of histogram for the number of 6s rolled?

Which word, *random* or *predictable*, better describes the behavior of the die as shown in the histogram?

What does the mean represent for the data set in the table above? What does it tell you about the probability of rolling a 6? Does the median provide similar information about the probability of rolling a 6? Explain.

Extend

Construct a histogram and calculate the mean and median for the data on the number of 6s collected by your class groups. How is your histogram similar to or different from the histogram for Ms. Feeney's class? How are your means and medians similar to or different from those of Ms. Feeney's class?

DEVELOPING
ACTIVITY 3-5

The Gumball Machine

A gumball machine contains 6 blue, 3 red, and 1 green gumballs. If you have no control over the way the machine dispenses gumballs, what color gumball are you most likely to get when you buy one gumball?

Investigate

List the possible gumball colors when a gumball is dispensed. What color do you predict is most likely to be drawn from the machine?

Set up a gumball machine by placing the appropriate number of marbles, counters, or similar objects in a box. Draw out one "gumball," record its color, and return it to the box. Do this 30 times in all, each time recording your results.

Share

Why was it necessary in this problem to replace the gumball in the box after each draw?

What do your results suggest about the gumball color that is most likely to be dispensed on a single draw from the machine?

Report to the rest of the class on your prediction and your experiment. Combine all of the data reported by your classmates. How often did each color come up for the combined class data? What does the combined class data indicate about the probability of getting each color?

Extend

Yuri suggests that blue is the most likely color to be dispensed and that its probability is $\frac{6}{10}$. How close is Yuri's probability to the probability for blue that you calculated from the combined class data? Would you have expected the two probabilities to be the same? Why or why not?

Another Look at Gumball Probabilities

Yuri suggested that blue is the most likely color to be dispensed from a gumball machine having 6 blue, 3 red, and 1 green gumballs. Yuri also claimed that the probability of getting blue was $\frac{6}{10}$. How could you justify Yuri's claim that the probability of drawing a blue gumball was $\frac{6}{10}$ without experimenting as you did in Activity 3-5: The Gumball Machine?

Investigate

Examine the following conversation between Jennifer and Rajan. They are discussing Yuri's claim about the possible outcomes from the gumball machine and their probabilities.

Jennifer: I think Yuri is wrong. The outcomes are blue (B), red (R), and green (G). Because they are equally likely, the probability of each color is $\frac{1}{3}$.

Rajan: I agree with Yuri! The outcomes are B B B B B B R R R G, and each of the ten gumballs is equally likely to be drawn. Because of this, blue (B) has a probability of $\frac{6}{10}$, red (R) has a probability of $\frac{3}{10}$, and green (G) has a probability of $\frac{1}{10}$.

Share

Who do you think is correct, Jennifer or Rajan? Justify your choice.

Julia agreed with Rajan, but she said that the probability of blue was $\frac{3}{5}$. Do you agree with Julia?

Extend

If you get a blue gumball on the first draw and chew it, has the probability of your getting a blue gumball on the second draw changed? Why or why not? Has the probability of your getting a green gumball changed after the first draw? Why or why not?

DEVELOPING
ACTIVITY 3-7

Modeling the Gumball Machine

How would you construct a spinner with three colors—blue, red, and green—so that it models drawing one gumball from a machine having 6 blue, 3 red, and 1 green gumballs?

Investigate

You have a choice of three spinners. One is broken into three identical parts, one broken into five identical parts, and one broken into ten identical parts. Choose a spinner and color it so that it will model or represent drawing a gumball from the machine.

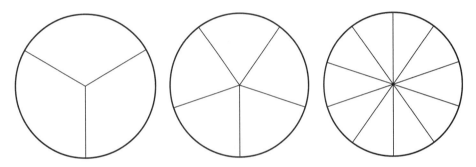

Share

Describe your spinner and explain why it works like the gumball machine. Be sure to talk about both outcomes and probabilities in your explanation.

Claire drew her spinner like the one shown here. Does it model a single draw from the gumball machine? Explain.

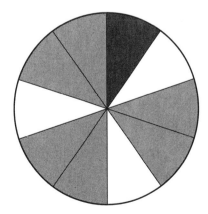

Extend

Does the spinner that you created continue to model the gumball machine when you make more than one draw from the gumball machine, chewing each gumball that you get? Why or why not?

DEVELOPING
ACTIVITY 3-8

Another Gumball Model

How would you use the random-number generator on your TI-80 to model a single draw from a gumball machine that contains 6 blue, 3 red, and 1 green gumballs?

Investigate

Amy said, "I found a way to model the gumball machine using my calculator. I used it to generate random numbers between 1 and 10, and I let numbers 1 through 6 be the blue gumballs, numbers 7 through 9 be the red gumballs, and 10 be the green gumball."

Here's what Amy did. Try it on your calculator.

Press **MATH** and use the right arrow key **▶** to go to **PRB**. Now press **5**. You should see **RANDINT(** your screen.

Amy then entered the least number she wanted (1), then a comma, then the greatest number she wanted (10), and finally a bracket. This showed on the screen like this: **RANDINT(1,10)**.

Amy then pressed **ENTER** once to generate a number between 1 and 10, which really represented a gumball and its color.

Share

Does Amy's model represent a single draw from the gumball machine? Why or why not?

Extend

Pam used the same random-number generator as Amy did. However, in her model she designated the number 1 to represent a green gumball, numbers 2 through 4 be the red gumballs, and numbers 5 through 10 be the blue gumballs. Does Pam's method model a single draw from the gumball machine? Explain.

Make up one more method, different from Amy's or Pam's, to model a single draw from the gumball machine using the random-number generator on your TI-80.

Flipping a Nickel and a Quarter

> If you and your partner flip a nickel and a quarter at the same time, what is the probability that you will get heads on both coins?

Investigate

List the possible outcomes when flipping a nickel and a quarter at the same time. If the pair of coins is tossed 30 times, how often do you predict that both coins will show a head?

Toss the nickel and the quarter 30 times and record the number of times each outcome you listed above occurred. How often did both coins show a head at the same time? Check your results against your prediction.

Share

Report to the rest of the class on your prediction and your experiment. Combine all of the data reported by your classmates. How often did both coins show a head at the same time? Was this what you predicted? Why or why not?

Extend

If you flipped the same quarter two times, what is the probability that you will get two heads? Why? How is it like the original problem posed above? How is it different? Devise an experiment to justify your thinking.

DEVELOPING
ACTIVITY 3-10

Nickel-and-Quarter Outcomes

In thinking about what happens when a nickel and a quarter are flipped at the same time, as in Activity 3-9: Flipping a Nickel and a Quarter, Marion said there are three outcomes, HH HT TT. Pam said there are four outcomes, HH HT TH TT. Is there a way to determine probabilities so that both Marion and Pam are correct?

Investigate

You can use the **RANDINT(** command on your calculator to model the tossing of a nickel and a quarter at the same time. Press **MATH** and use the right arrow key ▶ to go to **PRB**. Now press **5**. You should see **RANDINT(** on your screen.

Then enter **0** (to represent a head), a comma, then **1** (to represent a tail), and finally a closing parenthesis. You should see this on your screen: **RANDINT(0,1)**.

Press **ENTER** twice. The first value tells you the outcome for the nickel and the second value tells you the outcome for the quarter. For example, the screen here shows the nickel landed head (0) and the quarter landed tail (1). According to Marion's plan, the result is a head and a tail.

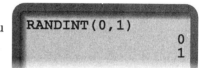

Repeat this process 30 times in all. Remember, you must generate two values each time to model the tossing of the nickel and the quarter. Record the results in two ways, one according to Marion's set of outcomes and a second according to Pam's set of outcomes.

Share

Report to the rest of the class the results of your experiment. Combine all of the data reported by your classmates in two ways, one according to Marion's set of outcomes and a second according to Pam's set of outcomes.

Is there a way to determine the probabilities for each of Marion's outcomes so that she is correct? Can you determine a set of probabilities for Pam's outcomes so that she is also correct?

When all the outcomes of an experiment have the same probability, the outcomes are said to be equally likely. Is each element in Marion's set of outcomes equally likely? What about Pam's? Explain.

Extend

Tim has a Kennedy half dollar. He tosses it twice. Write down the set of all possible outcomes for Tim's double toss so that all outcomes are equally likely. What is the probability that Tim's double toss results in one of each, that is, a head and a tail?

DEVELOPING
ACTIVITY 3-11

Music Time

Radio station TEEN claims that 50 percent of its air time is devoted to music. Ted heard this and wondered what would be the chance of hearing music, both times, if he turned on TEEN at two random times during the day. He decided to try this for several days. What is the probability that Ted will hear music both times?

Investigate

Predict how often Ted will hear music both times he turns on TEEN during the day. Place an X somewhere on the scale from 0 percent to 100 percent to indicate the percentage of the time Ted would hear music twice in one day.

Toss a nickel and a quarter to represent Ted turning on TEEN at two random times during the day. Use a head to represent *music* and a tail to represent *no music*. Do this 20 times to represent 20 days and record your results.

Share

Why does the tossing of a nickel and a quarter model Ted's turning on TEEN at two random times during the day? Talk about both the outcomes and their probabilities.

Report to the rest of the class the results of your experiment. Combine all of the data reported by your classmates and use that data to determine the experimental probability that Ted will hear music both times he turns on TEEN. How does this compare with your prediction?

Extend

Charles says that the probability that Ted will hear music both times he turns on TEEN is $\frac{1}{4}$ because it is the probability of getting two heads when a nickel and a quarter are tossed together. Is Charles correct? Why or why not?

Does Charles's probability agree with your experimental probability? Explain.

DEVELOPING

ACTIVITY 3-12

More Music

Radio station MUSO claims that $\frac{2}{3}$ of its air time is devoted to teen music. If you tune your radio to MUSO at a random time during the day, what is the probability you will hear teen music? Will the probability that you hear teen music change if you pick another random time in the same day? If you tune your radio to MUSO at two random times during the day, what is the probability that you will hear teen music both times?

Investigate

Predict how often you will hear teen music both times you turn on MUSO during the day. Place an X somewhere on the scale from 0 percent to 100 percent to indicate the percentage of the time you would hear teen music twice in a day.

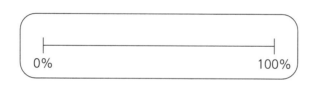

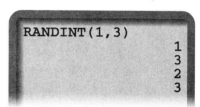

Enter **RANDINT(1,3)** on your TI-80. If necessary, refer to Calculator Help 9: Generating Random Numbers to access **RANDINT(**. This will generate one of three numbers, 1, 2, or 3, where 1 represents *music*, 2 represents *music*, and 3 represents *no music*. Use **RANDINT(1,3)** to generate 20 random pairs. The screen above shows two pairs. The first day produced (1, 3) where 1 represents *music* and 3 represents *no music*. The second day produced *music* (2) and *no music* (3). On neither of these two days did we hear teen music both times.

For the 20 random pairs you generated, determine how many times teen music occurred both times.

Share

Why do the pairs generated from **RANDINT(1,3)** model turning on MUSO at two random times during the day? Talk about both the outcomes and their probabilities. Why were the numbers 1 and 2 both assigned to music and only the number 3 assigned to no music?

Report your experiment results to your class. Combine the data reported by your classmates and use that data to determine the experimental probability that you will hear music both times you turn on MUSO. How does this compare with your prediction?

Extend

What other device could be used to model tuning randomly to radio station MUSO twice? Describe how you would use this device to solve the problem.

DEVELOPING
ACTIVITY 3-13

Shooting Free Throws

> Roger is practicing for the Koala Middle School basketball tournament. He has kept track of his shooting statistics and finds that he makes about 60 out of every 100 free throws. If Roger is at the line for two free-throw shots, what is the probability that he will make both of them?

Investigate

Predict how often Roger will make both shots by placing an X somewhere on the scale from 0 percent to 100 percent to indicate the percentage of the time Roger will make both shots.

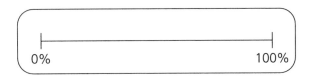

0%   100%

Use **RANDINT(** to model Roger's free-throw shooting. Given Roger's shooting record, what values will you use in the parentheses after **RANDINT(**? Which numbers, from the range you indicated in parentheses, will represent a free throw made? Which will represent a free throw missed?

Use **RANDINT(** and the numbers you selected to simulate Roger's shooting two free throws. Record whether or not Roger made both free throws. Repeat this simulation 30 times in all, noting the number of times Roger made both free throws. If necessary, refer to Calculator Help 9: Generating Random Numbers.

Share

What values did you use in the parentheses after **RANDINT(**? Why?

Would it have been possible to have chosen another set of numbers for this? Explain.

Why do the pairs generated from your simulation model Roger shooting two free throws?

What did your simulation data indicate about Roger's probability of making both shots? How does this compare with your prediction? How do your results compare with the complete set of class data?

Write a letter to a friend describing how you solved this problem.

Extend

Assuming the same shooting record for Roger, what is the probability that he will score exactly 1 point when he is on the line for a 1-and-1 free-throw opportunity?

DEVELOPING
ACTIVITY 3-14

Can a Coin Remember?

> Anna and Tim are playing a game that involves tossing a coin. Tim has just tossed a head. Anna says that the probability of getting a head on the next toss has decreased, because Tim has just tossed a head. Tim maintains that it doesn't make any difference. He says, "The probability of getting a head next time hasn't changed. The coin can't remember what it got last time." Who is correct? Why?

Investigate
What do you predict is the probability of tossing a head immediately after getting a head? Devise an experiment using a coin to test your prediction. Remember, you must look at the probability of getting a head immediately after a head.

Share
Describe your experiment. Explain why it helped you answer the question raised in Anna's and Tim's discussion.

What is your response to the question raised in Anna and Tim's discussion? Justify your response and compare it with the responses of other students.

Extend
Tim and Anna have tossed a coin four times. Which of the following outcome sequences is most likely to occur? Or are they all equally likely? Explain your choice.

A) H T T T
B) H H H H
C) T H T H
D) H H T T

DEVELOPING
ACTIVITY 3-15

What's the Chance of a Red Gumball?

> A gumball machine contains 3 red and 2 green gumballs. Ben wanted a red gumball. On the first draw he got a green gumball and placed it in his pocket for his sister who likes green gumballs. Ben wondered, "Has my probability of getting a red on the second draw changed?"

Investigate

Predict whether or not Ben's probability of getting a red gumball on the second draw has changed.

Devise an experiment to test your prediction. Use slips of paper or colored cubes to represent the gumballs in the machine. Be sure that your experiment enables you to find Ben's probability of getting a red on the second draw after getting a green on the first.

Share

Describe your experiment. Explain why it helped you compare Ben's probabilities of drawing a red gumball before he drew a green gumball and after he drew a green gumball.

Has Ben's probability of getting a red on the second draw changed? Why or why not?

How is Ben's problem with the gumball machine similar to or different from Anna's and Tim's problem with tossing a coin in Activity 3-14: Can a Coin Remember?

Extend

Mike says, "Ben's probability has not changed, because there are still 3 red gumballs in the machine." Explain how you would respond to Mike's comment.

DEVELOPING
ACTIVITY 3-16

Snow on the Flower Bed

Madi is watching large snowflakes fall in front of her house (see diagram below). What is the probability that the next snowflake will land on her flower bed? What is the probability that it will land on the driveway?

Investigate

What do you predict is the most likely location for the next snowflake? How likely is it that the flake will fall on Madi's flower bed? Show your predictions by placing marks on the probability scale shown here.

0%   100%

List the possible outcomes for the next snowflake to fall in front of Madi's house. You will need to calculate the area for each possible outcome (region) and then determine what fraction each is of the entire area in front of her house.

Share

How could you use areas to find the probability that the next snowflake will land on Madi's flower bed? Why do you think area is the appropriate measure to use for this problem?

Find the probability for each possible outcome. What is the sum of these probabilities? Is this what you expected?

Extend

Suppose the last snowflake landed on the grass. What is the probability that the next snowflake will not land on the grass?

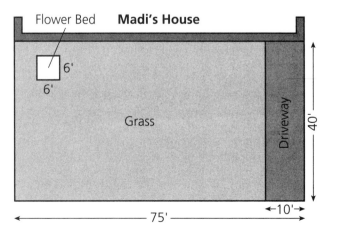

DEVELOPING
ACTIVITY 3-17

Rain on the Plain

Weather reports for Des Plaines forecast that there is a 50 percent chance of rain on Saturday and a 50 percent chance of rain on Sunday. What is the probability that it will rain on both days?

Investigate

Predict the probability that it will rain on both days. Show your prediction by placing a mark on the probability scale shown here.

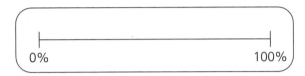

Wanda proposed this solution to the problem. Read it and discuss it with your partner.

"I marked 50 percent on a probability scale to show the chance of rain on Saturday. I then marked 50 percent on a second probability scale, arranged vertically, to show the chance of rain on Sunday (see a below). Because 100 percent is the greatest possible probability, I drew a square to show the whole area and then drew lines at each 50 percent mark (see b below). I shaded each 50 percent probability region, so the double-shaded part shows rain on both days (see c below). This area is $\frac{1}{4}$ the area of the entire region. This shows that the probability that it will rain both days is 25 percent."

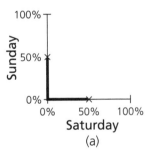
(a)

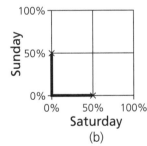
(b)

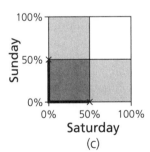
(c)

Share

How can you use a different method to solve this problem? Will your answer be the same as Wanda's?

Why does Wanda's method work? Share your explanation with your partner.

Extend

Weather Reports for La Cel forecast a 40 percent chance of rain on Saturday and a 60 percent chance of rain on Sunday. Explain how to determine the probability that it will rain on both days.

DEVELOPING
ACTIVITY 3-18

Too Much Rain on the Plain

Cindy is driving with her dad from Wallaby to Des Plaines, a distance of 60 miles. At some random time during Cindy's trip, a flash flood occurs at Inundate, a city 40 miles from Wallaby. If this flash flood results in delays for 5 miles on either side of Inundate, what is the probability that Cindy and her dad will be past the delay zone when the flooding occurs?

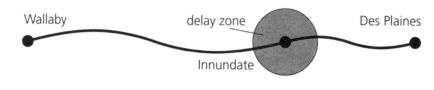

Investigate

Predict the probability that Cindy and her dad will be past the delay zone when the flooding occurs. Now show your prediction by placing a mark on the probability scale shown here.

On the diagram at the top, show all of the locations that are possible for Cindy and her dad when the flash flood occurs. Now show all locations that Cindy and her dad could have been if they were past the delay zone when the flash flood occurred.

How can this information be used to find the probability that Cindy and her dad will be past the delay zone when the flooding occurs?

Share

Describe how you solved the problem and explain why your solution is appropriate for this situation.

How is your solution strategy similar to the one you used for Activity 3-16: Snow on the Flower Bed? How is it different?

Extend

What is the probability that Cindy and her dad will be outside the delay zone when the flooding occurs?

APPLYING
ACTIVITY 3-19

Steffi Versus Monica

> In head-to-head professional tennis matches at the end of 1995, Steffi Graf led Monica Seles 7 matches to 4. Based on these data, which player is more likely to win their next match?

Investigate

Who do you predict will win the next match? Show the probability of your prediction by placing a mark on the probability scale.

0%   100%

Share

Write a letter to a friend to describe and explain how you solved the problem and found the probabilities for each player winning the next match. Tell your friend whether your probabilities are theoretical or experimental probabilities.

Extend

In the rivalry between Steffi Graf and Monica Seles, Steffi won the ninth and eleventh matches and Monica won the tenth match. Does this extra information change the probability that Steffi Graf will win the twelfth match? Why or why not?

Summer Music Time

> During the summer, radio station MUSO increases the amount of air time devoted to teen music to 80 percent. If you turn on your radio to MUSO at two random times during a summer day, what is the probability that you will hear teen music both times?

Investigate

What could you use to model tuning into MUSO?

Devise a simulation you can use to determine the probability that you will hear teen music both times you turn on MUSO during a summer day.

Carry out your simulation for 50 trials (50 days) and record the number of times that you heard music both times on the same day.

Share

Share your simulation process with your classmates. Explain how you found the probability that you will hear teen music both times you turn on MUSO during a summer day.

How were all the simulation processes shared in your class alike and how were they different?

Extend

What method, other than conducting a simulation, can you use to solve this problem? Compare your ideas with those of your classmates. Will you get the same results as you did with the simulation? Explain.

APPLYING
ACTIVITY 3-21

Have the Chances Changed?

Jody and Cameron are playing a game that involves rolling a die. Jody has just rolled a 6. Cameron complains that his chance of getting a 6 on the next roll is less because Jody has just rolled a 6. Jody says, "It doesn't make any difference what I got; the probability of getting a 6 next time hasn't changed." Who is correct? Why?

Investigate

What do you predict is the probability of rolling a 6 immediately after getting a 6? Devise an experiment to test your prediction. Remember, you must look at the probability of getting a 6 immediately after a 6.

Share

Describe your experiment. Explain why it helped you answer the question raised in Jody's and Cameron's discussion.

What is your response to the question raised in Jody's and Cameron's discussion? Justify your response and compare it with other students.

Extend

Jody and Cameron have rolled the die four times. Which of the following outcome sequences is most likely to occur? Which is least likely? Are any equally likely? Explain each choice.

A) 1, 5, 2, 4
B) 6, 6, 3, 1
C) 1, 2, 3, 4
D) 2, 4, 3, 6

APPLYING
ACTIVITY 3-22
The Windsurfer Race

In the Windsurfer Race Game, there are eleven windsurfers, numbered 2, 3, 4, 5, 6, 7, 8, 9, 10, 11, or 12. Two dice are rolled, and on each roll, the sum of the two dice is found. The windsurfer whose number matches the sum of the dice moves one space forward on the race board. The winner is the first windsurfer to cross the finish line, 10 spaces from the start.

Which windsurfer has the best chance of winning the game. Why?

Investigate

Which windsurfer number do you predict would win the game? Explain your prediction.

Work in pairs to simulate playing the game on the game board. One person rolls the dice, and the other move the windsurfer whose number matches the sum. Note which windsurfer number wins the game and where on the board the other windsurfer numbers finish.

For each windsurfer, write down the number combinations on the two dice that will allow that windsurfer to move forward one space. For example, the number combinations for Windsurfer 4 are 1 + 3, 3 + 1, and 2 + 2.

Share

How can you use the number combinations to determine the windsurfer most likely to win? Describe how you can use the number combinations to find the probability of winning for each windsurfer.

Explain to your partner why 1 + 3 and 3 + 1 were counted as two separate number combinations for Windsurfer 4?

Extend

Devise a similar game that uses the product of the numbers on two dice, rather than the sum. Write a letter to a friend describing the game and explain which windsurfer has the best chance of winning this game.

GAME BOARD FOR
WINDSURFER RACE GAME

START 1 2 3 4 5 6 7 8 9 10 FINISH

APPLYING
ACTIVITY 3-23

Getting a Green Light

> Juan's mother plans to drive him to school. Juan read in the local newspaper that the lights in his town are red 50 percent of the time, green 40 percent of the time, and amber 10 percent of the time. There are three lights between Juan's home and his school. Juan is about to set out for school. What is the probability that all three lights will be green as his mother approaches?

Investigate

Predict the probability that all three lights will be green.

Devise a method for solving the problem.

Share

Share your solution process with your classmates. Explain how you found the probability that all three lights will be green.

Compare your method with those of your classmates. How were they similar and how were they different? Did you all get the same result?

Extend

What is the probability that at least two of the lights between Juan's home and his school will be green?

APPLYING
ACTIVITY 3-24

Can You Guess the Secret Number?

Chandra is playing the Secret Letter Game at the Madison Middle School Fair. She was told that the secret letter was one of four letters F, A, I, or R. What is her chance of guessing the secret letter on her first try?

Chandra guessed F the first time, but was told she was not correct. She decided to try again. Did her chance of winning change on the second try? Why or why not?

Investigate   Devise a method for solving the problem.

Share   Share your solution process with your classmates. Explain how you determined whether the probability had changed for Chandra's second guess.

Compare your method with those of your classmates. How were they similar and how were they different. Did you all get the same result?

Extend   Construct a new Secret Letter Game in which the probability that Chandra will choose the correct letter the first time is $\frac{1}{20}$. Write two probability questions you can ask about this new Secret Letter Game. Answer your questions and give them to your partner to answer.

A Tied Election

> A school chess team needs to elect a captain and an assistant captain. Four people, Jason, Julie, Tim, and Anna, were nominated for captain and they all received an equal number of votes. In order to break the tie, the team coach decided to draw one name from a bag containing each of the four names. What is the probability that Anna will be chosen as the captain?
>
> If Julie's name is drawn for captain, and the coach then draws a name from the bag for assistant captain, what is the probability that Anna will be chosen assistant captain?

Investigate   Devise a method for determining the probabilities.

Share   Share your solution process with your classmates. Explain how you determined the probability of Anna being chosen captain and the probability of Anna being chosen assistant captain. Were these two probabilities different? Why or why not?

Devise an experiment you could use to check your results, and explain why your experiment works.

Extend   Suppose Julie is elected captain. Is the probability that a boy will then be chosen assistant captain greater than the probability that a boy will have first been chosen captain? Explain.

Extra Information in a Tied Election

> Another school chess team is electing a captain. Five people, Tom, Brett, Gabriella, Angela, and Susan, were nominated for captain and they all received an equal number of votes. In order to break the tie, the coach decided to draw one name from a bag containing each of the five names. What is the probability that Susan will be chosen captain?
>
> If the coach draws the name from the bag and announces it is a girl, has Susan's chance of being captain changed or is it the same as before? Why or why not?

Investigate   Devise a method for determining the probabilities.

Share   Share your method with your classmates. Explain how you determined the probability of Susan being named captain before knowing a girl's name had been drawn and the probability of Susan being named captain after it was known that a girl's name had been drawn. Did the two probabilities change? Why or why not?

Extend   Suppose that the coach announces that a boy's name has been drawn. What is the probability that Brett will be captain? Has his chance of being captain changed from what it was before the coach's announcement? Why or why not?

APPLYING
ACTIVITY 3-27

Eva at the Free-Throw Line

In a 3-shot free throw, Eva has a 50-50 chance of making the first shot. If she makes the first shot, her confidence grows and she has a 60 percent chance of making the second basket. However, if she misses the first shot, she has only a 30 percent chance of making the second basket. What is the probability of her making both free throws?

Investigate

Devise a method for determining the probabilities. You might consider using a simulation, the area approach taken in Activity 3-17: Rain in the Plain, or some other suitable strategy.

Share

Share your solution process with your classmates. Explain how you determined Eva's probability of making both baskets.

Extend

Eva's friend Isabel has a 70 percent chance of making her first free throw and a 90 percent chance of making the second if she misses the first. What is the probability that Isabel will miss both shots?

Can you find the probability of Isabel making both shots? Why or why not?

CHALLENGING
ACTIVITY 3-28

Lucky Number Combination

You are a contestant on a TV quiz show. To win the prize, you must guess the lucky three-digit number, where one digit is drawn from each of three boxes. The first digit will be drawn from Box A, which contains a 1 and a 2. The second digit will be drawn from Box B, which contains a 3 and a 4. The third digit will be drawn from Box C, which contains a 5 and a 6. Do you have a better chance of winning a prize or do you have a better chance of not winning a prize?

Suppose you guessed a 1 for the first digit and 1 was correct. The TV host is about to draw the number from Box B. Has your probability of winning the prize changed? Why or why not?

Investigate

Devise a method for solving the problem. Be sure to include a list of all three-digit numbers that are possible for the game.

On the scale below, show the probabilities of winning before and after the first digit was correctly guessed.

Share

Write an article for the bulletin board that describes and explains how you solved the problem.

Extend

For the Super Prize on the same TV quiz show, you win a prize by guessing the lucky four-digit number where one digit is drawn from each of four boxes. If the Boxes A, B, and C contain the same digits as before and the fourth, Box D, contains a 7 and an 8, what is the probability that you will win the Super Prize? What is the probability that you will win the Super Prize if you've successfully guessed the first two digits?

CHALLENGING
ACTIVITY 3-29

Which Die Numbers?

> Helen and Simon are playing a game in which a single die is rolled. If the die shows a 5 or a 6, Helen gets the number of points shown on the die, that is, 5 or 6, and Simon gets 0 points. If the die shows a 1, 2, 3, or 4, Simon gets the number of points that are shown on the die, that is, 1, 2, 3, or 4, and Helen gets 0 points. The winner of the game is the first player to have a total of 20. Who has the better chance of winning, Helen or Simon? Why?

Investigate

Predict who has the better chance of winning a game, Helen or Simon.

Play the game several times with a partner and record the winner of each game. Has your prediction changed? Why?

Share

Ross says, "Simon will win because he has four numbers while Helen only has two."

His partner, Zach, doesn't agree. He says, "Helen has the better chance of winning, because each number is equally likely and 5 + 6 make 11, while 1 + 2 + 3 + 4 is only 10."

Comment on these solutions. Is one solution more valid than the other? Explain your thinking and include a more refined explanation of the solution that you think is correct.

Extend

Suppose Helen and Simon now play the game with an 8-sided die, numbered 1 through 8. Ross suggests the game will be fair if Helen takes 7 and 8, Simon takes 1, 2, 3, 4, and 5, and neither player scores when a 6 is rolled. Is Ross's interpretation accurate? Why or why not?

Drawing for a Festival Ticket

Channel Island Middle School is holding its annual Fine Arts Festival. The table here shows the number of students, categorized by grade and gender, who are eligible to win a free family pass to the festival. The fine arts director announces the winning name to be Jenny Osborne. What is the probability that Jenny is in the seventh grade?

Channel Island Middle School	Boys	Girls
seventh graders	22	31
eighth graders	34	21

Investigate

Devise a method for solving the problem. It may be helpful to analyze the table of information.

Share

Share your solution process with your classmates. Explain how you determined the probability that Jenny is in the seventh grade. Did you all get the same result?

How was this problem similar to, as well as different from, Activity 3-26: Extra Information on a Tied Election?

Extend

Cindy said, "I made a mistake. I assumed that the fine arts director had announced that the winner was a seventh grader and I worked out the probability that Jenny won the family pass." Did it really matter?

APPENDICES

Data Sets

Calculator Helps

Glossary

Data Set 1

Tennis-Ball-Bounce Data

Elapsed Time (seconds)	Total Number of Bounces
0	0
10	12
20	24
30	36
40	48
50	60
60	72
70	84
80	96
90	108
100	120
110	132
120	144

Data Set 2

Colleen's Tennis-Ball-Bounce Data

Elapsed time (seconds)	Total Number of Bounces
0	0
20	24
40	48
60	72
80	96
100	120
120	144

Data Set 3

Sneaker Lengths and Sneaker Sizes

Name	Sneaker Length (cm)	Sneaker Size
Alberto	34	13
Amy	26	6
Andre	28	8
Ayako	29	9
Cam	29	9
Conchita	33	12
Goran	32	11
Hannah	32	11
Heather	28	8
Jennifer	27	7
Jim	29	9
Jodi	28	8
Karen	26	6
Kim	30	10
Kristina	24	5
Martin	24	5
Mike	32	11
Natalia	29	9
Roger	30	10
Sergio	33	12
Sophie	30	10
Stephanie	27	7
Taylor	28	8
Todd	32	11
Zac	27	7

Top-Grossing Rock-'n'-Roll Tours

Group	1995 Earnings (millions)	Group	1994 Earnings (millions)
Eagles	$65.6	Rolling Stones	$124.2
Boyz II Men	43.3	Pink Floyd	104.6
Grateful Dead	36.9	Billy Joel	75.8
R.E.M.	35.3	Eagles	73.7
Jimmy Page and Robert Plant	34.1	Barbara Streisand	58.9
Van Halen	34.0	Elton John	56.8
Tom Petty	28.1	Grateful Dead	48.8
Billy Joel and Elton John	22.8	Lollapalooza '94	27.0
Elton John (solo)	21.8	Phil Collins	26.2
Alan Jackson	17.3	Aerosmith	23.3

Data Set 5

Judges' Scores for Ice-Skating Competition

Judge Number	Caterina's Scores	Christie's Scores
1	8	10
2	7	8
3	9	9
4	9	6
5	7	7

Data Set 6

Middle-School Basketball Statistics

BLUEBIRDS' Basketball Statistics

Player Name	Points Scored	Personal Fouls	Time on Bench (minutes)
Angela	10	3	2
Monica	8	2	4
Juanita	6	1	4
Nicole	2	4	6
Rachel	7	1	2
Amanda	1	2	10
Putu	2	1	12

HAWKS' Basketball Statistics

Player Name	Points Scored	Personal Fouls	Time on Bench (minutes)
Jana	12	3	1
Gabriella	6	2	3
Julie	6	2	4
Cornelia	5	4	6
Steffi	9	1	1
Amanda	2	3	11
Mya	1	1	14

Data Set 7

Movie Running Times

Movie Title	Running Time (hours and minutes)	Number of Weeks Shown
Ace Ventura: When Nature Calls	1 hr 31 min	2
American President	1 hr 55 min	3
Assassins	2 hr 13 min	3
Balto	1 hr 18 min	1
Casino	2 hr 50 min	4
Cutthroat Island	2 hr 3 min	2
Dracula: Dead and Loving It	1 hr 30 min	3
Father of the Bride II	1 hr 46 min	4
Four Rooms	1 hr 37 min	3
Gold Diggers	1 hr 33 min	2
GoldenEye	2 hr 9 min	5
Grumpier Old Men	1 hr 41 min	6
Heat	2 hr 52 min	2
Jumanji	1 hr 44 min	6
Now and Then	1 hr 42 min	3
Sabrina	2 hr 4 min	3
Sudden Death	1 hr 50 min	4
Tom and Huck	1 hr 33 min	2
Toy Story	1 hr 21 min	5
Waiting to Exhale	2 hr 3 min	4

Data Set 8

Population Density and Unemployment in 10 US Cities

City	Population	Area (square miles)	Percent Unemployment
Albuquerque	384,619	136	6.4
Atlanta	393,929	131	8.3
Buffalo	328,175	42	10.7
Chicago	2,783,726	228	9.0
Corpus Christi	257,428	104	8.6
Dallas	1,007,618	333	7.7
Grand Rapids	189,126	43	7.6
Houston	1,626,902	556	8.8
Los Angeles	3,485,557	465	10.9
Miami	358,648	34	11.1

Calculator Help 1

ENTERING LISTS

1. Select a list location for your data.

   • Press **STAT**.

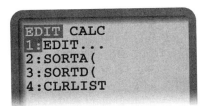

   • Under the EDIT menu, press **1**, or alternatively, highlight **1:EDIT . . .** and press **ENTER**.

   • Use **◄** and **►** to move among the lists L1, L2, . . . , L6. In the illustration here, we have selected list L1 for the data.

2. Clear the list if necessary.

   • Use the arrow keys to move the cursor to the top of the list to be cleared. On the screen shown here, we have moved to the top of list L1. Note that a formula for the list is echoed on the bottom line of the screen.

   • Press **CLEAR**. Observe the disappearance of the right-side expression in the formula at the bottom of the screen. Press **ENTER**. The selected list is now empty, with the cursor on the first line of the empty list.

3. Enter data into the selected list.

   • Key in each data value, pressing **ENTER** each time.

Tips

   • As you enter a data value, it is echoed on the bottom line of the screen.

   • Other information at the bottom of the screen shows you the current location and contents of the cursor. From the first data-entry screen, **L1(4) = 165** indicates that the cursor is in list L1 and is positioned on line 4. The value 165 will be stored in location L1(4) when you press **ENTER**.

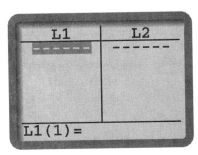

For more information turn to pages 9-9 to 9-12 in the TI-80 Guidebook.

SORTING LISTS

1. Confirm that the data have been entered into a list.

   • Press [STAT] and then press [1] or [ENTER].

   • Use [◄] and [►] to move among the six lists in search of your data. The screen here shows sneaker lengths from Data Set 1 stored in list L1.

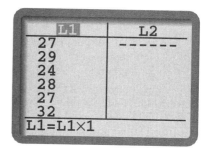

2. Sort the data in list L1 from least to greatest value.

   • Press [2nd] [LIST] then press [1] or [ENTER].

   • Press [2nd] [L1] and then press [ENTER]. The TI-80 will display **done** when the ascending sort is completed.

   • To sort data in another list, follow these steps, changing L1 to the appropriate list name (L2, L3, . . .).

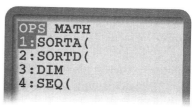

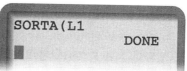

3. Sort the data in list L1 from greatest to least value.

   • Press [2nd] [LIST] and then press [2] or, alternatively, press [▼] and [ENTER].

   • Press [2nd] [L1] and then press [ENTER]. The TI-80 will display **DONE** when the descending sort is completed.

4. Return to the list to view your sorted data.

   • Press [STAT] and press [1] or [ENTER].

   • Use [◄] and [►] to move among the six lists in search of your data. The screen here shows the sneaker lengths ordered from longest to shortest.

For more information turn to page 8-6 in the TI-80 Guidebook.

HISTOGRAM

1. Set the range.

   - Press WINDOW.
   - Key in values for XMIN, XMAX, XSCL, YMIN, YMAX, and YSCL. XMIN, XMAX, YMIN, and YMAX are the minimum and maximum values for *x* and *y*, and XSCL and YSCL are the intervals on the *x*- and *y*-axes. Press ENTER after each entry to move to the next line.

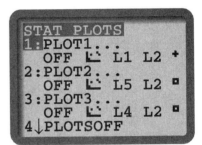

2. Define the histogram.

   - Press 2nd STAT PLOT
   - Press 1 or press ENTER to display the plot 1 menu.
   - Press ENTER to turn on plot 1.
   - Press ▼ to access the type options.
   - Press ▶ three times to highlight the histogram icon ⬛. Press ENTER.
   - Press ▼ to access the **XL:** options. If your data are in L1, press ENTER. Otherwise, use ▶ to highlight the list containing your data and press ENTER.
   - Press ▼ to highlight the **F:** (frequency) options. If your frequency is 1, press ENTER. Otherwise, use ▶ to highlight the list containing your frequency and press ENTER.

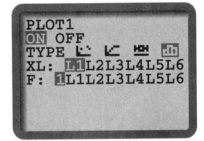

3. Display the histogram.

   - Press GRAPH.

Tips

   - Key in window values before defining and plotting the histogram.
   - In setting the window, set XMIN at or below the smallest data value and set XMAX at or above the greatest data value.
   - Set XSCL to 1 if the width of each bar in the histogram is to be 1 unit. Otherwise, set XSCL to the desired width for each bar of the histogram.
   - Set YMIN equal to 0 and set YMAX to exceed the largest count (frequency) of any class interval.

For more information turn to pages 9-19 to 9-21 in the TI-80 Guidebook.

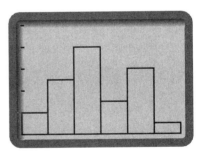

BOX PLOT

1. Set the range.

   - Press WINDOW.

   - Key in values for XMIN, XMAX, XSCL, YMIN, YMAX, and YSCL. Press ENTER after each entry to move to the next line.

2. Define the box plot.

   - Press 2nd STAT PLOT

   - Press 1 or press ENTER to display the plot 1 menu.

   - Press ENTER to turn on plot 1.

   - Press ▼ to access the type options.

   - Press ▶ twice to highlight the box plot icon ▦. Press ENTER.

   - Press ▼ to access the **XL:** options. If your data are in L1, press ENTER.Otherwise, use ▶ to highlight the list containing your data and press ENTER.

   - Press ▼ to highlight the **F:** (frequency) options. If your frequency is 1, press ENTER. Otherwise, use ▶ to highlight the list containing your frequency and press ENTER.

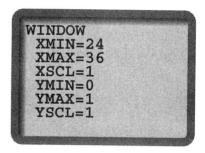

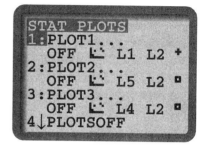

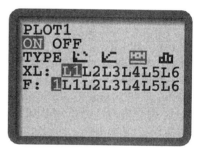

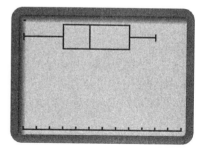

3. Display the box plot.

   - Press GRAPH.

Tips

   - Key in window values before defining and plotting the box plot.

   - In setting the window, set XMIN at or below the least data value and set XMAX at or above the greatest data value.

   - The window values for YMIN and YMAX do not affect the position of the box plot on your screen.

   - Set XSCL to a desired horizontal scale to help interpret the box plot.

For more information turn to pages 9-12 to 9-21 in the TI-80 Guidebook.

Calculator Help 5

1-VARIABLE STATS

1. Confirm that the data have been entered into a list.

- Press STAT and then press 1 or ENTER.

- Use ◄ and ► to move among the six lists in search of your data. The screen here shows 1995 earnings from Data Set 2 stored in list L1.

2. Calculate 1-Variable Statistics for the data in list L1.

- Press STAT and then press ► to highlight **CALC**.

- Press 1 or ENTER to select **1-VAR STATS**.

- Press 2nd L1 .

- Press ENTER . The 1-variable statistics for the data in list L1 are displayed on the screen.

For more information turn to pages 9-14 and 9-15 in the TI-80 Guidebook.

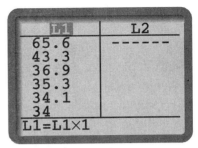

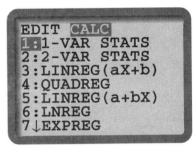

SCATTER PLOT

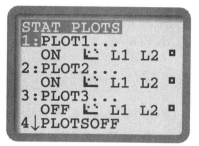

1. Here, we have used list L1 for the first variable data (*x*) and list L2 for the second variable data (*y*). The ordered pairs (*x, y*) represent time on the bench and points scored for the 14 middle-school basketball players listed in Data Set 4.

2. Turn on the stat plot, indicate plot type, and identify data location.

   - Press **2nd** **STAT PLOT**. Use the arrow keys to highlight **1:PLOT1...** and press **ENTER** or, alternatively, press 1.

   - To turn on **PLOT1**, highlight **ON** and press **ENTER**.

   - To indicate plot type, on the **TYPE** line highlight the first icon, **⊾**, and press **ENTER**.

   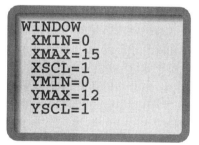

   - To indicate location of x data, on the **XL** line highlight L1 and press **ENTER**. To indicate location of *y* data, on the **YL** line highlight L2 and press **ENTER**.

   - On the **MARK** line, highlight your choice of point marker to appear on the scatter plot and press **ENTER**.

3. Adjust window dimensions.

   - Press **WINDOW**.

   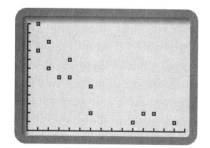

   - Key in values for XMIN, XMAX, XSCL, YMIN, YMAX, and YSCL. Use the smallest and largest values in the two lists to help determine XMIN, XMAX, YMIN, and YMAX. Press **ENTER** after each entry to move to the next line.

4. Display the scatter plot.

   - Press **GRAPH**.

For more information turn to pages 9-18 and 9-20 in the TI-80 Guidebook.

ENTERING FRACTIONS

1. To represent a proper or improper fraction,

   - Enter a numerator.
   - Press [2nd] [b/c].
   - Enter a denominator.
   - Press [ENTER].

2. To represent a mixed number,

   - Enter a whole number.
   - Press [2nd] [Unit ⌐].
   - Enter a numerator.
   - Press [2nd] [b/c].
   - Enter a denominator.
   - Press [ENTER].

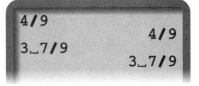

3. To compute with common fractions,

   - Enter common fractions together with operator symbols. The screen here shows $\frac{1}{3} + \frac{1}{5} = \frac{8}{15}$, $\frac{2}{5} \div \frac{1}{2} = \frac{4}{5}$, and $3\frac{1}{7} - 1\frac{1}{10} = 2\frac{3}{70}$.

Tips

- The calculator is factory-set to express results as mixed numbers. To express results as improper fractions, press [MODE], arrow down to the fourth line, highlight **b/c**, and press [ENTER]. Exit the mode screen by pressing [CLEAR] or [2nd] [QUIT].

- The calculator is factory-set to automatically simplify common fractions to lowest terms. To force manual simplification, press [MODE], arrow down to the fifth line, highlight **MANSIMP**, and press [ENTER]. Here, $\frac{1}{3}$ and $\frac{4}{8}$ have been entered. Note the symbol ↓ preceding $\frac{4}{8}$ indicating that the fraction can be simplified. To do so, press [FRAC], highlight **1:>SIMP**, and press [ENTER]. The fraction is simplified and the common factor is shown. Press [ENTER] again to continue simplifying.

For more information turn to page 1-11 and chapter 3 in the TI-80 Guidebook.

LINE DRAWING

1. Create a scatter plot on your screen.

   • See Calculator Help 6: Scatter Plot.

   • The plot here shows population density (x) and percent unemployed (y) using Data Set 6. The scatter plot window is shown for your use.

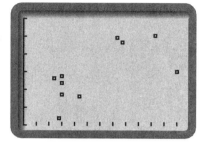
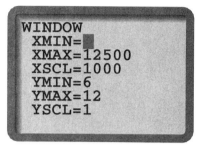

2. Access the line draw command.

   • Press 2nd DRAW.

   • Press 2, or, alternatively, use ▼ to highlight **2:LINE(** and press ENTER. You will see the scatter plot with a flashing crosshair at the middle of the screen and (x, y) coordinates at the bottom of the screen.

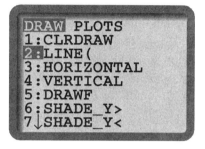
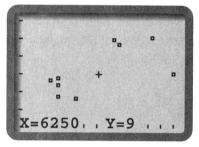

3. Draw a line segment on the plot.

   • Use the arrow keys (◄, ►, ▲, ▼) to move the flashing crosshair to the point at which you want to place one end of a line segment. Note the readout of the (x, y) location of the flashing crosshair.

   • Press ENTER to anchor one end of the segment. The flashing crosshair is now surrounded by a box. On the screen shown here, the flashing crosshair is in the solid box.

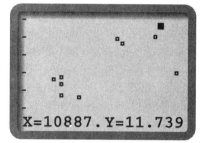

   • Now use the arrow keys to move the flashing crosshair to a point at which you want to place the other end of the segment. The segment is created as you move the crosshair.

   • Press ENTER to anchor the entire segment.

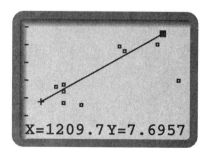

4. Return to step 2 to draw additional segments.

For more information turn to page 7-4 in the TI-80 Guidebook.

GENERATING RANDOM NUMBERS

1. Access the probability menu.

   • Press MATH and press ▶ two times to highlight **PRB**.

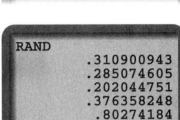

2. Generate a random number between 0 and 1.

   • Press 1 or ENTER to select **RAND**.

   • Press ENTER. A random number between 0 and 1 appears on the screen.

   • Continue to press ENTER to generate additional random numbers between 0 and 1.

   • Press CLEAR to clear the screen.

3. Generate a random integer between two specific values.

   • Under the **PRB** menu (first screen above) press 5 or, alternatively, use ▼ to highlight **5:RANDINT(** and press ENTER.

   • After the left parenthesis, enter two integers separated by a comma and then a right parenthesis.

   • Press ENTER. A random number between the two integers (inclusive) appears on the screen.

   • Continue to press ENTER to generate additional random numbers between the two integers.

   • Press CLEAR to clear the screen.

For more information turn to pages 2-12 and 2-13 in the TI-80 Guidebook.

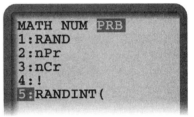

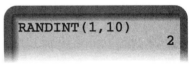

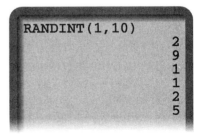

GRAPHING A FUNCTION

1. Enter the function to be graphed.

   - Press Y= .

   - Key in the function.

2. Adjust the viewing window.

   - Press WINDOW .

   - Key in values for XMIN, XMAX, XSCL, YMIN, YMAX, and YSCL. Press ENTER after each entry to move to the next line.

3. Display the graph.

   - Press GRAPH .

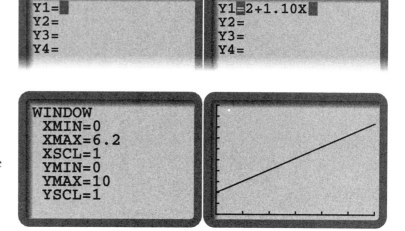

Tips

- Up to four functions can be entered for simultaneous graphing.

- Use ▲ , ▼ , or ENTER to move among Y1, Y2, Y3, and Y4 under the Y= key.

- Use the (−) key to indicate negative values for window dimensions.

- Constants, stored values, and arithmetic manipulations can be entered as window dimensions and scale values. For example, pressing 2nd π ENTER places an approximation for π into the window, and pressing 5 x² places 25 into the window.

- Functions may be stored under the Y= key for later use. To store a function without plotting it, move the cursor on to its equal sign and press ENTER to deselect that function's graph. If the equal sign is highlighted, the function's graph will be displayed.

For more information turn to page 4-1 in the TI-80 Guidebook.

CREATING A TABLE

1. Enter one or more functions to be used in creating a table.

   • Press Y= .

   • Key in up to four functions.

2. Set up the table values.

   • Press 2nd TblSet .

   • Key in a value for **TBLMIN**.

   • Press ENTER and key in a value for Δ**TBL**.

3. Display the table.

   • Press 2nd TABLE .

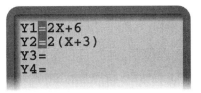

Tips

   • Review Graphing a Function for more information on entering functions.

   • **TBLMIN** controls the first x-value to be shown in the table. Δ**TBL** controls the constant change in x that will be shown in the table. Δ**TBL** can be negative.

   • Six data pairs (x, y) are visible on the screen. The value highlighted by the cursor is echoed on the bottom line of the screen, perhaps with greater precision than shown in the table.

   • Use ▲ and ▼ to scroll above and below the six data pairs that first appeared in the table. Use ◄ and ► to shift from the independent variable values x to the dependent variable values y. If more than one function has been entered and selected under the Y= key, use ◄ and ► to shift among the dependent variable values of the selected functions.

   • Press 2nd TblSet again to change **TBLMIN** and Δ**TBL**. When you first return to the table setup menu, **TBLMIN** echoes the x-value last shown at the top of the table.

For more information turn to page 6-1 in the TI-80 Guidebook.

Glossary

additive change a change in a relationship based on a constant addition from one term to the next; the terms 3, 5, 7, 9, . . . show an additive change.

axis one of the number lines of a coordinate grid

base in an exponential expression, the number to be raised to a power; in 4^3, 4 is the base and 3 is the exponent.

bivariate data *see* two-variable data

box plot (box-and-whiskers plot) a visual summary of a data set where a box is used to represent the middle 50 percent of the data, and line segments stemming from the box are used to represent the bottom and top 25 percent; the line segments are often called the whiskers.

center of a distribution one or more of the representative values that anchor a distribution on a number line. The mean, median, and mode are typically used as centers of a distribution.

class one of the equal-length intervals used in a histogram

cluster an obvious grouping of data values within a data set

coefficient in a linear function, the number by which x is multiplied; in $y = 2x + 3$, 2 is called the coefficient of x

complement an event composed of all sample space outcomes not in the given event; when a die cube is rolled, the complement of the outcome $\{2, 4, 6\}$ is the outcome $\{1, 3, 5\}$

conditional probability a probability statement based on a restricted sample space; when a die is rolled, the conditional probability of getting 6 given that the roll is even is $\frac{1}{3}$.

constant slope a slope that never changes; in a linear relationship, the slope is constant.

decay factor in an exponential relationship, the multiplicative factor between 0 and 1 that determines the rate of decay; in the expression $y = \left(\frac{3}{4}\right)^x$, the fraction $\frac{3}{4}$ is the decay factor; also called the decay rate.

dependent events two or more events whose outcomes depend on each other

dependent variable a variable whose value depends upon the value of one or more variables

dispersion a measure of the spread in a data set, as indicated by range, IQR, and standard deviation

distributive property a property of numbers a, b, and x, such that $ax + bx = (a + b)x$ and $x(a + b) = ax + bx$

ellipse a geometric shape resembling an oval having two lines of symmetry

ellipse test the use of an ellipse to capture all points in a scatter plot of a data set to suggest whether the data exhibit a trend

equally likely outcomes outcomes with the same probability, or likelihood, of occurrence

equation a mathematical sentence equating two expressions

equivalent equal

event a set of possible outcomes

expected value a weighted average based on a probability experiment. In a game in which you get 3 points for a die roll of 6, and 0 points otherwise, your expected value is $\frac{1}{6}(3) + \frac{5}{6}(0) = 0.5$; on the average, you get 0.5 points per roll.

experimental probability probability expressed as the ratio of the number of successful trials to the total number of trials

exponent in an exponential expression, the power to which a number is raised. In 4^3, 4 is the base and 3 the exponent.

exponential relationship a relationship involving an exponential expression in which the independent variable is the exponent. The relationship $y = 2^x$ is an exponential relationship.

expression a mathematical phrase that uses numbers, variables, and operation symbols to represent a value

extrapolate to make a prediction that extends beyond the data set; compare to interpolate.

five-number summary a set of five position markers including the maximum and minimum data values, the upper and lower quartiles, and the median

frequency the number of times an item occurs in a set of data, or the count for a particular item in the data set

function a relationship in which there is exactly one value of the dependent variable for any given value of the independent variable

gap an obvious space between values in a data set

growth factor in an exponential relationship, the multiplicative factor greater than 1 that determines the rate of growth. In the expression $y = 2^x$, the value 2 is the growth factor; also called the growth rate.

histogram a graph of a frequency distribution in which the width of the bars corresponds to the class width and the height of each bar is the frequency for that class

independent events two or more events whose outcomes do not depend on one another

independent variable a variable whose value determines the value of a dependent variable

intercept a point on an axis that a graph crosses or touches

interpolate to make a prediction within the range of a data set, compare to extrapolate

interquartile range (IQR) the difference between the upper quartile (the seventy-fifth percentile) and the lower quartile (the twenty-fifth percentile)

line of best fit a line that is best, or is seen to be best, in representing a trend in a data set

linear relationship a relationship between two data sets represented by a straight-line scatter plot and has an equation in the form $y = mx + b$

lower fence a point that is below the lower quartile by a distance 1.5 times the IQR; it is the division point for lower outliers.

lower quartile the median of the lower half of a data set, also called the twenty-fifth percentile

mean the arithmetic average of a set of values; found by dividing the sum of the values by the number of values

median the middle number in a set of data values when the values are listed in order, also called the fiftieth percentile. When there are an even number of values in a data set, the median is the arithmetic average of the two middle values.

mode the value or values of a data set that occur most frequently

multi-variable data a data set that contains more than one value data for each element in the set

multiplicative change a change in a relationship based on a constant multiplier from one term to the next; the terms 1, 2, 4, 8 . . . show a multiplicative change.

non-linear relationship a relationship between two data sets that cannot be represented by a straight-line scatter plot and cannot be represented be an equation of the form $y = mx + b$.

normal distribution a mound-shaped, perfectly symmetrical distribution, in which the median, the mean, and the mode have the same value

one-variable data a data set that contains one value for each element in the set

outcome a possible result in a probability experiment

outlier one or more extraordinary values in a data set, set off or away from the rest of the set; *see* upper fence and lower fence

parabola a curve resulting from a quadratic relationship $y = ax^2 + bx + c$.

percentile a value corresponding to a position in a data set based on percentage; if the value 15.4 is the fortieth percentile, then 40 percent of the data values are at or below 15.4 and 60 percent are at or above 15.4.

probability a number that tells the likelihood or chance of an event; it is represented by a number from 0 to 1 inclusive.

quadratic relationship a relationship whose graph is a parabola; a relationship expressed in the form $y = ax^2 + bx + c$

RANDINT(a TI-80 calculator function used to generate random integers from a particular set

random number a number in which each of the digits zero through nine have an equal probability of being selected for any position in the number. Tables of random numbers can be used to simulate experiments.

range the difference between the greatest and least values in a data set

rate of change a ratio of the change in the dependent variable for a given change in the independent variable

raw data a data set in its original form

sample part of a population upon which an experiment or survey is conducted

sample space a list of possible outcomes

scatter plot a two-dimensional coordinate graph of individual points

ΣX a TI-80 symbol representing the sum of all the x values

simulation modeling a probability situation by generating and analyzing random outcomes

slope the rate of change in a relationship

spread *see* dispersion

standard deviation an index used to describe the spread in a data set based on the distance from the mean of the elements in the data set.

STAT PLOT a description of the type of graph to be shown on the calculator

success a favorable outcome in a probability experiment

SX a TI-80 symbol representing the standard deviation of the sample

symmetrical distribution a distribution with a mirror or reflection line at its midpoint; a normal distribution is symmetrical.

theoretical probability probability based on symmetry, numerical composition, geometrical properties, or other probability calculations

TRACE a TI-80 feature that allows you to display values from a plot on the TI-80 screen

tree diagram an organized list of all possible outcomes of a probability experiment

trial an attempt to carry out an event in a probability experiment

truncate to remove a portion of a number based on decimal place

two-variable data a data set containing two values for each element in the set

upper fence a point that is above the upper quartile by a distance of 1.5 times the IQR. It is the division point for upper outliers in a set of data

upper quartile the median of the upper half of a data set, also called the seventy-fifth percentile

variable a quantity that changes

whiskers in a box plot, the segments from the ends of the box to the maximum and minimum values

$\bar{x}$ the symbol for mean, also called *x-bar*

XMAX the value in a TI-80 graph `WINDOW` that determines the largest possible *x*-value to be shown

XMIN the value in a TI-80 graph `WINDOW` that determines the smallest possible *x*-value to be shown

XSCL the value in a TI-80 graph `WINDOW` that determines the distance between tick marks on the *x*-axis to be shown on the graph

YMAX the value in a TI-80 graph `WINDOW` that determines the largest possible *y*-value to be shown

YMIN the value in a TI-80 graph `WINDOW` that determines the smallest possible *y*-value to be shown

YSCL the value in a TI-80 graph `WINDOW` that determines the distance between tick marks on the *y*-axis to be shown on the graph